More Parable

By the Same Author

Parables for Now

MORE PARABLES FOR NOW

Edmund Flood

Illustrated by Penelope Burns

Dimension Books · Denville, New Jersey

First USA edition published by Dimension Books, Inc.

First published in Great Britain in 1981
Darton, Longman and Todd Ltd
89 Lillie Road
London SW6 1UD

© 1981 Edmund Flood
Illustrations © 1981 Darton, Longman and Todd Ltd

ISBN # 0-87193-192-3

British Library Cataloguing in Publication Data

Flood, Edmund
  More parables for now.
  1. Jesus Christ – Parables
  I. Title
  226'.8'06   BT375.2

  ISBN 0–232–51532–8

Contents

CHAPTER 1 Parables   1

CHAPTER 2 Our Relationship With God   3
    The Friend at Midnight   4
    The Unjust Judge   9
    The Unmerciful Servant   15
    The Servants Entrusted with Money
    (The Talents)   23

CHAPTER 3 People, Possessions and Ourselves:
    How We Need To See Them   29
    The Good Samaritan   31
    The Rich Fool   40
    The Rich Man and Lazarus   47
    The Pharisee and the Tax-Collector   56

CHAPTER 4 The Time Is Now   62
    The Servant Entrusted with Supervision   63
    The Hidden Treasure and *The Pearl*   67
    The Shrewd Steward   73

CHAPTER 5 The Choice   80
    The Children in the Market Place   81
    The Wicked Tenants   86

CHAPTER 6 Impressions   90

ENDNOTES   93

Acknowledgement

Except where otherwise indicated, biblical quotations are taken or adapted from the Jerusalem Bible, published and © 1966, 1967 and 1968 by Darton, Longman and Todd Ltd and Doubleday and Co. Inc., and are used by permission of the publishers.

CHAPTER 1 Parables

Stories, like clothes, are used for many purposes. When Jesus was telling his stories he knew it was at a time of urgent opportunity. Human history, he believed, had come to its turning-point. Would people be able to recognize the gift he had to offer them?

He had to help those around him see behind the unimpressiveness and even scandal of his life to what he knew was in him. Through his stories they might not only catch what he *felt* about the situation, but also understand it.

In his parables Jesus shows the real significance of his actions. Suppose you took his meals with the rejected, and instead of being shocked by them, held them up against that centuries-old promise that God would one day gather together his scattered people. Jesus' story of the *Lost Sheep* gave his listeners the opportunity of doing that. It was asking them to take another look at Jesus' evident joy in dining with 'sinners'. For who was the shepherd in this story: God or Jesus? And, looked at in a clearer light, wasn't this a joy in which the listener would give anything to join?

And if you *did* join him: what then? What should a true follower of Jesus do, and what blind alleys should be avoided? It is Jesus' parables on those questions that concern us in this book. In another book I considered the parables Jesus told about himself and about what it's like to be with him. In this book we look at the practical consequences of joining Jesus. We could call it the Christian agenda.

In each parable Jesus gave his listeners a bit of Palestinian life and asked them to enter into the incident sympathetically, as we might when watching a play. In one parable they were asked to feel how it was to be a beaten-up man lying by the roadside, in another to enter into the feelings of a labourer who quite unexpectedly had the chance of great wealth, or in another those of a person who felt affluent and secure.

Now what experience in your own life does this experience I've just made up for you illumine? That was the question Jesus raised by telling a parable.

For a parable is a question, not a statement. It leaves your dignity of making your own decisions intact. All it tries to do is to help you make those decisions with greater sensitivity by giving you a similar kind of experience on neutral territory, where you're less likely to feel you're being got at.

So to find what Jesus wants to say to us in a parable we have first to reconstruct the bit of life he described and see what kind of situation that was originally meant to throw light on. Then it will be what Jesus intended it to be: not a grand, remote statement, but a lively piece of human communication on a matter of importance to us all.

Once we have it in all the penetrating liveliness of its original challenge, we can use it to illuminate our own lives. As possible helps to that, a few reflections are added to each commentary. More detailed questions are discussed in the Notes, but they are intended only for readers who wish to explore the parable further.

Jesus told his parables as homely tales to homely people. Today, as never before, scholars have made it possible for us to recapture their original simplicity, and consequently their charm and power.

A word, finally, on how this book is arranged. For each parable I give a reconstruction of the original text so far as possible, then a commentary, and a few reflections that may be of some help to those who wish to reflect on the parables prayerfully. Notes on some more detailed points follow for those who want a fuller kind of explanation. Technical explanations, designed only for the specialist, are buried at the back in the form of endnotes. The superior (¹) numbers in the text refer to these endnotes.

CHAPTER 2 Our Relationship with God

The Friend at Midnight
The Unjust Judge
The Unmerciful Servant
The Servants Entrusted with Money (the Talents)

Those who join Jesus are involving themselves in the coming of God to the world. But where is this God? Does he listen? All of us wonder about that from time to time, especially when everything goes wrong. In his stories about the *Friend at Midnight* and the *Unjust Judge*, Jesus offers his answer.

Then, what kind of God is this? What is our fundamental experience of him? The *Unmerciful Servant* parable takes us to the very heart of our humanness and begs us to consider the implications.

The story of the *Servants Entrusted with Money* (or the *Talents*) takes us further into this relationship. What is God's attitude to what I am doing? What does he want of me? The story takes us back to our experience of any loving relationship that was real.

'Can any of you imagine having a friend and going to him at midnight and saying to him, "Friend, lend me three loaves, for a friend of mine has arrived on a journey and I have nothing to set before him," and the friend answering him from within, "Don't bother me. The door is now closed and my children are in bed with me, so I can't get up and give you anything."?

I tell you that even if he will not get up and give it him because of his being his friend, at least his desire to avoid disgrace will make him get up and give him whatever he wants.'[1]

Today it is unusual to have to ring a friend's doorbell at midnight to get a snack for a traveller who has just dropped in. But once we place this story in the Middle East setting where you might well travel by night to avoid the intense heat, it starts to become easier to visualize the scene.

A man arrives at a village about midnight at the end of that day's journey and calls at the house of a friend to ask for hospitality. He could count on getting what he needed. Hospitality was regarded as a sacred duty, not only on the part of the individual approached but also on the part of the village as a community.[2]

So the traveller's friend receives him with oriental courtesy and then turns his attention to providing a meal that will do justice to the high standard of hospitality expected of any self-respecting person and village. Of course there will be food in the house, since that is stored on a yearly basis in the raised loft at the end of a peasant family's one-room dwelling.[3] But he would be expected to put before his host an unbroken loaf of bread, and a spare one as well, and only the families who had baked very recently could be certain to have that.

His wife would know who had baked that day, and he could count on his neighbours' unwillingness to sacrifice the honour of the village, to be confident of getting the loaves from a family who had them.

Of course you didn't offer your guest just bread. A meal mainly consisted of an assortment of dishes into which everyone dipped pieces of bread from their loaves. These dishes would also have to be found, and some of them at least might have to be borrowed from the neighbours. But the host in Jesus' story decides to start with the most modest request possible: he asks his friend only for the loaves.

Now can you imagine that friend bluntly saying 'No' in those circumstances? Jesus asks. Would he blurt out 'Don't bother me', not even addressing him as 'friend'? Would he make a song and dance about opening the door or waking the children, who even if they *did* wake would quickly return to sleep?[4] And would he really say, 'I can't give you anything'?

A ridiculous suggestion for any self-respecting villager! *Friendship*, Jesus concedes, might not stir the man to help. Letting down a friend is common enough. But any villager could imagine the repercussions of saying 'No' to a request for a few loaves in those circumstances. Just imagine the host going on round the village asking others to help because 'that churlish fellow up the street let me down when all I was asking for was a loaf for an unexpected guest'! Everyone knew the gravity of that kind of social sin and the social punishment it would bring. For the dishonoured person, life in the village would be intolerable. So *of course* the man will give the host, not just his modest request for a couple of loaves, but 'all he needs'.

Honour, then, is the subject of this story. Even if you can't always count on the claims of friendship, surely you can count on your fellow-villager's need to preserve his or her essential self-respect?

And Jesus, by telling the story, seems to be asking his listeners whether the same wouldn't be even more true of God. If a villager could never think of becoming for the rest of the village 'the one who refused the means of hospitality', could God, the lover of his people, ever think of becoming for his friends 'the one who couldn't be bothered'?

The reason you can count on God, Jesus is saying, isn't just because of his feelings of friendship for you, but because of his very self-integrity. Could there be a stronger ground for confidence than that?

REFLECTION

All of us, sooner or later in our lives, need reassurance. Perhaps someone we love, or we ourselves have a serious illness, or a plan we rely on is frustrated. We can have the feeling, at times, that everything is going wrong, or that nothing really matters any more, or that no one cares for us. In one way or another, the world goes black and dead. So perhaps we turn to God. But even that can seem empty too. Religion can't change things, we decide.

And perhaps 'religion' doesn't change things. We don't get that job we had set our heart on; our best friend betrays us and is unrepentant; or we have a terminal illness and eventually we shall die. God was all right when things were going well, but when we really need him he might as well not be there.

Look around you, Jesus says to us in this parable. What, in your experience, is the most dependable thing about people? Self-preservation, yes; but that's something more than merely physical. Each of us has to preserve *our sense of self-hood*: the personality that makes us the kind of person we see ourselves as being. Just as that host, as he walked down the village street to the dark house of his sleeping friend, knew that it was of the very nature of things in a village that help would be given, so we, as we walk in light or in dark, should know that in the very nature of things God is for us. That is the kind of 'village' or world we inhabit: where, whatever happens, God will be true to his own self. It's no accident that when, in our own century, a non-Christian, Robert Bolt, asked himself what he found the essential quality of the man he particularly admired in *A Man for All Seasons*, it was Thomas More's being, yes, supple, humorous, unassuming and sophisticated, but above all in his being utterly true to his own self.[5]

The most reassuring thing about this parable is what we see here about the way Jesus communicated with people. He could simply have said, 'Stop worrying: you can depend on God.' Instead he puts before his listeners an incident in the village life that they knew so well and asks them, with a smile, a question about it. 'What do you think? Judge this by your own experience. Can any of us imagine . . .?'

He says nothing about God and his Kingdom; again that's left to the listener. 'Does this story help us to understand something essential about God? You must decide that, and not from my say-so, but from the shared experience of God's people.'

They knew about that, as we too can know it. From the beginning of that long relationship between God and his people, when God had revealed himself to Moses as 'the faithful God' (Exodus 34: 6), the God who always proves himself dependable, down the years, in all the mess and turmoil of life, song after song had celebrated that consciousness.[6] This is what they had known about God. But now a stronger proof was here. When John came to sum up what people had experienced in Jesus, he could only express it in terms of that revelation to Moses: Jesus, he said, was 'full of faithfulness': the dependability of God that we have 'seen with our eyes and touched with our hands' (1 John 1: 1).

NOTES

I. We are meant to imagine ourselves as being the person who needs the bread, not as the person from whom the bread is requested (though the New English Bible takes the opposite view).

II. The parable turns on an assurance that you can rely on the fact that the request will be granted for one reason. That reason, therefore, is the hinge of the whole piece. But unfortunately there is disagreement as to what the reason is. Even more unfortunately, many of the English versions present the reason as 'importunity' or 'persistence',[8] while it seems probable that the parable is concerned with something more fundamental than repetition. It is on what that fundamental thing is that disagreement comes. The problem arises from the fact that the text simply says that the friend will help 'because of his non-shame', but doesn't make clear whether this 'non-shame' is that of the host or of his friend, so that this key question has to be settled from our knowledge of other factors.

In the commentary I have adopted the view that the parable hinges on *the friend's* desire and need to be without shame, since 'the parable is centred on the attitude of the man in bed . . . and v. 8 is offering a contrast to the attitude expressed in v. 7.'[9] He needs to preserve his sense of honour, integrity, selfhood; and for him not to meet the kind of request made of him here would be to forfeit that.

It has recently been argued that the awoken friend met the request because of *the host's* non-shame: the 'shameless' or brazenly confident way in which the host makes the request of him. Evidence for this view is found in the fact that 'in Asia friends do not make requests with the preface "Please". It's the proof of friendship to ask as if the thing requested were the property of the asker. "Give me. . ." is the correct manner of asking.'[10]

Unfortunately the advocate of this view doesn't show cognizance of the strong arguments given above for the opposite view. Also, the parable says that if one means fails, an *alternative* means will succeed. But it is difficult to see how, if the awoken man will not give the food for motives of friendship, the host's acting as though they are real friends would provide that genuine alternative. In fact the proponent at times veers, perhaps unconsciously, towards the other view: 'The first factor of Asian friendship is the understanding "Your honour shall be my honour" . . . if he refuses, his own self-respect is endangered.'[11]

THE UNJUST JUDGE   Luke 18: 2–8

'There was a certain judge in a particular town who had neither fear of God nor respect for men. In that town there was a widow who kept on coming to him and saying, "Please take up my case against this person who owes me money." For a long time he refused, but at last he said to himself, "Maybe I have neither fear of God nor respect for man, but since she keeps pestering me I must give this widow the help she is entitled to, or her persistent coming will damage my reputation."

You notice what that unjust judge had to say? Now will not God give help in their need to his chosen who constantly cry to him, he who restrains his anger* against their sins? I tell you he will rescue them speedily. But when the Son of Man comes, will he find faithfulness on earth?'[1]

Jesus's story starts with a woman in an apparently impossible situation. Someone has defrauded her of money.[2] She can get it back only by going to law, and so she applies to the local judge to have her case heard. The implication of the story may be that he was well known in the village as 'a tough nut to crack'.[3] He turned down the woman's application.

She applied again and again; but it looked like a pebble against a mountain. The judge knew what the Bible said: 'Let none of you wrong his neighbour, but fear God.'[4] But he didn't 'fear God', so the rights of his neighbour meant nothing to him.

It looked a particularly hopeless case since the applicant was a widow. She wasn't necessarily old, since people nor-

---

* "Restrain his anger" is a catch-phrase Jesus took from the Old Testament, as the commentary will explain.

mally married between 14 and 16, and many people died young. But a widow was without a protector, especially in legal matters, and she tended to be held in low esteem.[5]

The helplessness of the widow made the judge's responsibility still more serious. Care for the helpless and oppressed was God's constant demand of his people. They must be like him: kind and faithful; and the Bible spelt out clearly what that entailed:

> God, forever faithful,
> gives justice to those denied it,
> gives food to the hungry,
> gives liberty to prisoners.
>
> God restores sight to the blind,
> straightens the bent,
> protects the stranger,
> keeps the orphan and widow.
>   (Psalm 146: 7–9)

God promised to be with his people only 'if you do not exploit the stranger, the orphan and the widow.'[6]

This judge ignored these demands. Even the law's requirement that he give precedence to a widow's case[7] he disregarded. The only law he recognized was what suited him.

The widow kept on at him; but for a long time he held his ground. Then at last he was beaten. He was overcome not by conscience but by a threat to his own prestige. Her continual knocking on his door for justice would blacken his reputation in the neighbourhood. He had to give in; and she got her request.

Jesus asked his friends to compare that situation with their own. They were longing for God's full coming: 'May your Kingdom come' was their constant prayer. But nothing seemed to happen. Instead of victory there was rejection and persecution. As with that widow, their prayers for help came to nothing.

Even in the way Jesus made the comparison between their situation and the widow's he gave a hint that things *were* changing. That decisive 'I tell you' had the ring of a God-like authority. Not in political change but in the very presence of that person who was speaking to them was their wish being granted.[8]

And what is this person's message to those who constantly beg for God's help and seem to get nowhere?

Part of his message came from the way he had told that story. In his story a proverbially helpless person got justice through sheer persistence even from a godless judge. But he told it in such a way that its structure and phrases repeatedly echoed a description his audience would have known of a very different kind of judge: 'The Lord is a judge, who is no respecter of persons. . . . He listens to the plea of the injured party. He does not ignore the orphan's supplication, nor the widow's as she pours out her story.'[9] If persistence will get you justice in the end and even from a godless judge, how

much more certain that you will get it from *that* kind of judge!

The other part of Jesus' message came from his reminding them of how God treats his chosen people. He had offered them a two-way relationship. They could respond to his love or reject it. He would always be faithful; but to benefit from this they must be faithful too. If they remained loyal to him, he would always be compassionate. There would be suffering, as a result of the evil they had done, but not the overwhelming suffering that their evil deserved. God would, in his love for them, limit the consequences for them of that evil: he would 'restrain his anger' in view of their faithfulness and prayer.

Jesus' audience knew from their Bibles that that was the kind of relationship they had been offered by God. By using the catch-phrase 'restrains his anger', Jesus was deliberately reminding them of its central features. As lovers know, a relationship has much to do with feeling. As we hear the Bible's descriptions, we enter into that feeling as well as catching the echoes that Jesus was deliberately setting up:

> God, who does what is right,
> is always on the side of the oppressed. . . .
> He is tender and compassionate,
> *restraining his anger*, most loving. . .
> he never treats us, never punishes us,
> as our guilt and our sins deserve.
> No less than the height of heaven over the earth
> is the greatness of his love for those who fear him. . . .
> As tenderly as a father treats his children,
> so God treats those who fear him,
> as long as they keep his covenant
> and remember to obey his precepts.
>   (Psalm 103: 6–18)

We hear the same refrain[10] in another Bible prayer:

> You are my God, take pity on me, Lord,
> I invoke you all day long;
> give your servant reason to rejoice.
>
> Lord teach me your way,

how to walk beside you faithfully.

Lord God, you who are always merciful and tender-hearted,
restraining your anger, always loving, always loyal,
turn to me and pity me.
Give me your strength, your saving help.
                    (Psalm 86: 3–16)

By using that catch-phrase as the climax of his parable
Jesus was reminding his listeners of those immensely en-
couraging descriptions of God's way of acting with us. How
different from the judge in my story; though even he gave
in in the end! And don't those descriptions ring with confidence, that God who is loving and compassionate will help
his chosen people in their trouble? All he asks is that you
trust in him, are faithful to him, and that you are open and
ready for his coming. The delay in his giving you his full
help, the full coming of his Kingdom, will be short. In the
meantime, like one always loving and loyal, he will treat the
evil you do with compassionate restraint. But already in me
you hear his authoritative voice. In my coming you should
recognize the imminence of the Kingdom. How important
that you should be as persistent in your faithfulness to God
as that widow was in her quest for help, or my coming will
be of no avail to you.

REFLECTION

1. As always, Jesus relies on the background of the Jews'
experience of God. So to understand the parable we need to
let it bring back to us the poetry in which they tried to
express their experience. We may decide to reflect quietly on
the three passages from the Psalms given in the commentary.
Who is the God who makes and guides our world and whose
Kingdom Jesus knew he was bringing? And what does he
want from us?

2. Jesus' long experience of village life had taught him how
much a widow could need help and protection and how deaf

some local judges could be to the pleas of the powerless. Through the parable he tries to help people in an everyday experience that he understood just as well: people trust in God and beg him to help them, but nothing seems to happen.

Jesus invites us here to reflect on several things when we feel like that. Above all, as we've just seen, there is what countless men and women who have been faithful to God have experienced of him. Then there is what we know from our experience of life of the need for faithfulness to those we love and of what that sometimes entails. But these basic realities are made more powerful here by the sympathy and the understanding of ordinary life that Jesus shows here and by the authoritativeness of his assurance that the God he knew so well would so obviously do better than that ruffian judge. He would rescue his chosen and this would happen speedily, with the coming of the Son of Man.

Do we find that assurance, trust and enthusiasm infectious? If so, we shall want to be 'merciful, tender-hearted, always loving, always loyal', as realistically as such an attitude was needed by that widow. And not because we feel obliged to, but because we know who it is that is with us and because we want to walk beside him faithfully.

THE UNMERCIFUL SERVANT
Matthew 18: 23–34

'The Kingdom of God may be compared to a king who decided to settle his accounts with those who served him. When the reckoning began, they brought him an official who owed ten thousand talents; but he had no means of paying, so his master gave orders that he should be sold, together with his wife and children and all his possessions, to meet the debt. At this, the official threw himself down at his master's feet. "Give me time," he said, "and I will pay the whole sum."

The king had compassion on him, so he let him go and cancelled the debt.

Now as the official went out, he happened to meet a colleague who owed him one hundred denarii; and he seized him by the throat and began to throttle him. "Pay what you owe me", he said.

His colleague fell at his feet and implored him, saying, "Give me time and I will pay you." But the other simply said he wouldn't; on the contrary, he had him thrown into prison till he should pay the debt.

Other colleagues of his reported the whole affair to their master, and he sent for him. "You wicked servant," he said, "I cancelled all that debt of yours when you appealed to me. Were you not bound, then, to have compassion on your colleague just as I had compassion on you?" And in his anger the master handed him over to the torturers till he should pay all his debt.'

A Middle-Eastern ruler summoned the governors of his provinces. As the men for collecting the taxes from extensive areas in their master's kingdom, they handled large sums of money; and their sense of power, and their remoteness from the capital, could encourage them to forget that they were only servants of the king and so to keep some of the taxes for themselves.

At the meeting it became clear that one of the governors owed the king a sum that is so enormous that to describe it Jesus simply takes the largest unit of currency and the highest number used in currency.[1] He wanted to indicate that the size of the man's debt to the king was 'out of this world'!

But though the debt itself was of 'science fiction' dimensions, the king's plan for dealing with it was entirely realistic. Jewish law allowed a creditor to sell into slavery a bankrupt debtor and his children, so that he could recoup part of the debt from the sale. It wasn't regarded as particularly cruel or vengeful, but simply as the only way one might be able to recover part of a bad debt. In fact if the proceeds from the sale would be greater than the debt, one wasn't allowed to take this step. Jewish law forbade the sale of the wife. But this was permitted by the less humane laws of other Middle Eastern countries known to Jesus' listeners.

The governor, facing this appalling predicament, takes the only course open to him. With the elaborate manners of an oriental, he prostrates himself before his king and begs for time.

Jesus seems to be hinting at this point in the story that the governor was asking the king for a quite exceptional kind of restraint. The word he uses for 'begs for time' is one often used in the Old Testament for the mercy shown by God himself to his own people:[2] not grudging, not self-complacent, but the kind that could prompt this cry of confidence and affection:

Lord God, you who are always merciful and tender-hearted,
restraining your anger, always loving, always loyal,
turn to me and pity me.
Give me your strength, your saving help.
(Psalm 86: 15–16)

What may be no more than a hint in the governor's request becomes a certainty when we are told the king showed him 'compassion' – a word then used almost exclusively of God and the Messiah.[3] It's like God's reaction to the unfaithfulness of his people:

> In excess of anger, for a moment I hid my love for you.
> But with tender kindness, I have compassion for you.
> The mountains may depart,
> the hills be shaken,
> but my tender kindness for you will never be shaken,
> and my covenant of peace will never be shaken,
> says God, the compassionate.
> (Isaiah 54: 8–10)

By now Jesus' listeners will have caught the drift of the story. The king was clearly meant to remind them of God's compassion for human weakness and sin, and they're therefore not surprised to hear that in answer to the governor's plea for time the king gives him what he hadn't dared to ask for: the cancellation of that enormous debt.

Folk-tales tend to work through contrasts, and Jesus' story follows the usual pattern. Just as the governor was leaving the king's palace after this extraordinary experience, he came across a colleague who owed him a sum that was precisely one-millionth of the debt just cancelled. Although his manner of arresting him may have been normal procedure, the rest of the account clearly underlines the complete contrast with the king. The debtor before him falls at his feet and begs for the same kind of God-like restraint that would give him time to pay. How can someone who has so recently felt an identical despair not have compassion for such a person? Surely he will forgive this small debt as he has just been forgiven that huge one?

The listener's expectation is dashed with brutal abruptness. The creditor gives no reason for denying the request. There is just a flat, 'I won't.' He can't sell his colleague as a slave, because, as we have seen, the law allowed that only if the debt was as great as the amount such a sale would raise; and the debt in this case was trifling. So he has him put into prison until he has earned the amount of the debt, either by the work he does there, or by his relations and friends paying the debt for him. Jewish law forbade such a step; but it was acceptable in other Middle-Eastern countries.

News of this was quickly brought to the king, and the story now reaches its climax.

To understand what Jesus is trying to do here we need to distinguish between the 'stage furniture' and the main action. The parable ends with dreadful punishment, and this can have greater vividness than what the king says, as well as making us wonder whether this 'compassionate' king was really as kind as the story claims.

Here we have to remember that on the level of a story about an oriental king, the listeners would have wanted to know what happened to the official when the king heard that he had so grossly abused the immense generosity shown him. They would have expected to hear of stern punishment. When forming his Gospel, Matthew tended to warn his Christian community of the consequences of sin by painting vivid pictures of punishment, so that he may have heightened the colours at this point in the story. Torture was employed in the Middle East (though not in Palestine) to discover where debtors had hidden their money or to persuade relations or friends to pay. But now that the king had withdrawn his earlier pardon for the gigantic debt, the process could be long.

We saw earlier in the story that what now seem brutal reprisals, like selling a whole family into slavery, were no more than part of the set of a Middle-Eastern tale. And this allows us to see where the real thrust of the conclusion lies. Typically of Jesus, it lies in *a question*: 'Were you not bound, then, to have compassion on your colleague, just as I had compassion on you?'

It certainly wasn't law that 'bound' him, but simply the experience he had undergone. He had known what it is to be accepted for the person one actually is: the person that heredity, environment, upbringing, good will, and, yes, inexcusable failures have made us all: not an acceptance of patronizing contempt or grudging forbearance, but one that is warm, tender and compassionate.

Once he has had that experience, everything in the story turns on whether he will allow it into his consciousness of himself and of others. And isn't it the same, the parable says, with the Kingdom? People claim to find God in many places. But we know that love can be found only by those who accept it.

REFLECTION

The parable raises a question that touches the very heart of our humanness. If you have known what it is to be human: to need love for the person you are and to receive it, what are you denying if you turn your back on that experience in the way you live? Are you denying, cancelling out, yourself?

This question is posed by the story to everyone, follower of Jesus or not. But in the context of his listeners' experience of him, and of their ancestors' long experience of God, it had an uncanny force.

Jesus' joyful parties with the tax-collectors, the door left wistfully open even to the Pharisees who sought to annihilate all he stood for, showed that Jesus took compassionate forgiveness as much for granted as the air he breathed.

He did so because he knew this to be the atmosphere of the Kingdom. If I go along to a great match or a wedding party believing that the human race is hateful and contemptible, then I cannot enter into the joy of the occasion, and you will say that my presence is merely physical. If I call myself a follower of Jesus and don't take an attitude of compassionate forgiveness for granted, can I expect to have a part in the coming of the Kingdom? Can I sincerely say 'Thy Kingdom come' if I don't also say with equal sincerity 'Forgive us our debts as we forgive those in debt to us'? Is that why Jesus said 'Be compassionate, as your Father is compassionate' and 'Happy the merciful, for they will obtain mercy'?

Jesus knew as well as any of us that we normally prefer a very different arrangement. I realize that I have done harm to people, but I generally keep this thought well away from my attention. And this has two consequences. First, I keep God out of my life as it really is. I forget that it is me as I am, 'debts' and all, that he wants to embrace and have with him in the coming of the Kingdom. Refusing to be myself, and so rejecting his compassion, I come to God simply with my 'good side'. I offer him not myself, but my merits.

And isn't it the same with our relationship with other people? I come home from work and my wife is bad-tempered. Immediately I feel affronted. Haven't I worked hard throughout the day and had an uncomfortable journey home? Don't I deserve gentleness and even appreciation?

Much worse than a passing storm at the end of a working day are settled attitudes. I love my job or a sport or playing a musical instrument and am considered quite good at them, but my husband is entirely indifferent. Or I paint the bathroom or cook the lunch and get no thanks. How shall I react?

One way is to feel the hurt but to retire into a feeling of superior aloofness. All right, he or she doesn't appreciate me. This only reinforces my exclusive attention to my strength. It is the other who has faults. And I regard them with a self-complacent coldness.

Or perhaps I realize that coldness is wrong and I try to take a 'Christian' attitude. I won't let this defect in my partner spoil our relationship. It's a pity the defect is there, but I shall be tolerant and forgiving.

Always it's *I* who am the creditor. I'm the one with rights: rights with God, since my merits have earned his favour; or rights with other people for my talents, strengths, and kindnesses to get the appreciation they deserve.

At the end of Jesus' parable he takes the governor at his word. 'You claim your rights,' Jesus says, 'well here's your balance sheet. Surely you could have realized that it shows a debt you can't repay?'

So the parable tells us that the Kingdom is an invitation to be true to our experience of God as the one who loves each of us for who we are. It invites us to consider whether someone who has experienced the freedom and hope brought by God's loving acceptance can fail to want to offer that to others.

NOTES

I. The Jewish religion of Jesus' time tended to view the relation to God as a legal and business relation, which was naturally expressed in terms of debt or credit. The relation with God was therefore something external: a transfer of merits and rewards.

In this parable Jesus puts forward a totally different understanding of this relation. We don't meet God at the other end of a telex in an interchange of debits and credits, but when we become aware of ourselves as we really are. Where else could I find God, the fulness of life, than at the heart of my actual life? And what else could the Kingdom be for me than living out the partnership I find there?

II. Folk-tales share the characteristic of their cousins, ballads and country dances, of relying for much of their effect on having a simple, easily recognizable structure. This has at least two important consequences for the effect of this parable if we look carefully at its three sections.

(a) The first of these becomes clear if we compare the first and second sections. Each falls into three parts:

an intended action (of settling accounts with a debtor)

his begging for time in words that are virtually identical so that for all their despairing urgency they seem to have something of the air of a refrain

then, after that almost lulling refrain, a sharply phrased contrast that the Greek makes prominent by placing the word for 'having compassion' immediately after the first refrain.

In this way the structure helps to show that the first two sections are principally concerned to contrast 'having compassion' and 'I won't.'

(b) The other result of looking carefully at the structure is that it helps us to notice where the stress lies in the third, climactic section. In the second and third sections again there is a refrain, that tells us that the debtor was sent for punishment 'until he should pay back the debt'. Even though the one at the end of the third section has probably been 'tuned up' by Matthew, the Greek words used in both are very similar. The fact that the punishment piece in each section is refrain enhances the impression that the king's speech is the *real* climax. This impression becomes still stronger when we remember that the first and second sections turn on a contrast between two psychological attitudes: 'having compassion' and 'I won't.' The third, climactic section is, as we might have expected, about exactly the same thing, though expressed not as an event but as a question: 'In these circumstances don't you feel obliged to show compassion?'

THE SERVANTS ENTRUSTED WITH MONEY (THE TALENTS)
Matthew 25: 14–30; Luke 19: 12–27.

'A man decided to travel to a distant country. Before his departure he summoned his three servants and gave to each of them a portion of his possessions. A long time later he returned, and he again summoned his servants, this time to give an account of their stewardship.

Two of the servants had done successful business with the capital that had been entrusted to them. Their master congratulated them and entrusted them with a still larger sum.

But the third servant had buried the money and so had made nothing with it. When asked to give an account of himself he sought to justify himself by pointing to his master's well-known hardness in business dealings. That had made him frightened, and so he had decided to take no risks.

His master took him at his own word. "In that case," the master told him, "you should at least have deposited the money in the bank, so that on my return I would have been able to get it back with interest." And the master punished that servant by taking away from him the money he had entrusted to him and giving it to the first servant.'

Matthew and Luke, as we shall see, used this story for their own purposes, and, as a result, made it rather complicated. But the version above is probably that of Jesus.[1]

Gone, we notice, is the billion-dollar handout. We are left with something far more down-to-earth. In fact we are left with money as we handle it every day, and the kind of responsibilities and opportunities it brings. As every bank manager knows, the farmer, the businessman, the shop-owner can generally use that extra bit of money *as an opportunity*: to develop the farm, the business or the shop's potential still further.

Of course money often means very different things to that, like buying the necessities of life or catching up with one's debts. But in Jesus' story the servants would already have had their everyday needs provided, and the money was given, not for them to stop gaps in their financial affairs, but to use positively. Their master had placed in their hands something powerful and dynamic.

What would they decide to do about it? Since the focus is on their decision, the story-teller withdraws the master from the scene. Then, a long time later, he returns to see what their decisions were.

Two of them, we are told, had used the money properly, and, in the way folk-tales have, the third will be a contrast to the other two. Already we are asking ourselves what the story is getting at. We know that Jesus wasn't in the habit of giving lessons in elementary economics! *He had come to announce the Kingdom.* As soon as we remember that, it all becomes clear and magnificent.

The gift is the one that Jesus was offering and that his followers had so joyfully accepted: the gift of taking part in the coming of the Kingdom. And the Kingdom, the story suggests, isn't something that just happens to you. It's something put into your hands. It's a gift, and it has great power. You have to decide how to use it; the person who gave it to you won't interfere. He will be delighted at your successes. But he wants them to be *your* successes, not just his.

REFLECTION

1. A vivid and lively reminder that life is a gift. The stress isn't on our obligation to the giver, but on the gift as a great opportunity. The giver has thrown it to us for us to get on with because he values our becoming more richly ourselves.

But we've heard so often that our Christianity is a 'gift' or a great opportunity that we may nod approvingly without recognizing what it entails. The parable tries to help us over this difficulty by comparing our role in the Kingdom with an opportunity of a specific kind. We all know that if a businessman wants to exploit his opportunities, whole-hearted involvement, courage and enterprise will normally be necessary. Do I need to revise my understanding and practice of Christianity in the light of this parable? Is it asking me to look with fresh eyes at the atmosphere I help to create in my family or at work, or the support and concern I give to people?

2. Is this one of the finest portraits of God in the Bible? He delights in what we do, not because we follow a book of rules, but because we are true to ourselves and the gift of creative life within us. Jesus' experience of God, that he

conveys to us here, isn't of a cop in a supermarket but of an enthusiastic supporter on the touchline.

3. So by means of simple imagery – money given to you and me to use – the parable puts our selves, with all our powers, and in all our freedom to choose, to explore and to build, at the centre of the picture in God's work for the world. There is no area of our lives, joyful or sad, that it cannot invest with new hope.

But maybe we can't see this. We know that we are largely creatures of our upbringing and our environment. If we haven't experienced love and trust, how can we recognize them in God? The third servant in Jesus' story believed his master was a hard man.

But it isn't for that that he is punished. His master blames him not for a defective understanding but for being false to himself. True he didn't realize that his master would take a real delight in his vigorous exploitation of the money. He felt obliged to protect himself from his master by taking no risks. But he did know that capital should be exploited. This was taken for granted by Jews of the time, and the servant doesn't dispute it. Had he deposited the money with the bank, he would have fulfilled *both* of his requirements, safety *and* profit.

The parable is saying that it's just the same with the Kingdom. A wrong understanding of God and what it's like to be with him is bound to limit our involvement in his Kingdom. But we should at least see that our life is a responsibility, even if we can't recognize that we have been given it by our Father and his joy and trust in what we do. If we do not respond even to that, then what capacity have we shown for fellowship with God, or even for a genuinely human life? Is the removal from the third servant of the money entrusted to him just a detail necessary for the structure of the story (a reward or a punishment has to be provided for each servant) or is it a hint of the possibility for each of us of moral and human bankruptcy?

NOTES

I. Matthew and Luke preserve basically the same central story and several roughly similar formulations, but each has developed it with considerable freedom for his own purposes. However important these purposes were in the circumstances of their times, the developments that arose from them have partly shifted the emphasis from the nature of the gift to the threat of punishment. The original parable seems to have arisen from a magnificent understanding of the Kingdom of God: as a gift that of its very nature (not because of fear of punishment) demands joyful and responsible exploitation. But Matthew and Luke, in their preoccupation with the final coming of Jesus, naturally saw the return of the master as an allegory for that coming and the accompanying final judgement, and this to some extent overshadows the original insight.

II. Matthew uses the parable to help warn his readers to 'stay awake, because you do not know either the day or the hour, *for* it is like a man on his way abroad. . .' (the 'for' is omitted in the *Jerusalem Bible* and the *New English Bible*). While Jesus' starting-point was a possible bit of business life, Matthew tends to jump that stage and go directly to the spiritual gifts of the Christian community. Hence he speaks of the impossibly large sums of a talent, and he tells us that these were given to each 'in proportion to his ability' (v. 15). What particularly weakens the force of the original parable is that the qualities of the servants seem not so much to *arise from* their response to the gift as merely to be shown by it. We're being invited to witness not how one becomes a true follower of Christ but how an already established moral standpoint (of 'good and faithful' or 'wicked and lazy') is demonstrated.

III. Luke wanted to use the parable to help show his readers that they shouldn't expect 'that the kingdom of God was going to show itself then and there' (v. 11); though this isn't in fact brought out firmly in his version of the actual story. Like Matthew, Luke has exploited the story's obvious potential for allegory. In his original telling of the parable, Jesus and some at least of his audience would have appreciated that the coming of the story's master to reward or punish on moral grounds was strikingly similar to the awaited coming of the Son of Man. But Matthew and Luke tend to make what was originally merely an implicit allusion into an explicit and principal teaching[2] so that the emphasis is less on the gift we have of the Kingdom than on final punishment or reward.

The change was, of course, a natural one, given the awareness that the whole of future history was pregnant with the future coming of the Son of Man. Luke, in his version of the parable, introduces another strand of that awareness: not merely will the Son of Man be a judge, he will also be the one whom the Jews so tragically rejected. This additional strand is expressed by modelling the master on Archelaus, who, on the death of Herod, went to Rome to claim the Jewish kingdom but found his claims opposed by a delegation of Jews. The two strands don't fit perfectly with one another, because Luke preserves the small sums of everyday life of the original story (a sum equivalent to about three months' wages rather than the billion-dollar 'talent' of Matthew)[3] and combines this with the huge reward of several cities. Luke has increased the number of servants to ten – to make it a more kingly allegory. The king's final command to 'bring them here and execute them in my presence' was of the kind not uncommon among kings. While Matthew's third servant had buried the money in the ground, Luke's had hidden it in the scarf used to protect the back of the head from the sun. Both were common Jewish practices; but the former was regarded as much safer.[4]

CHAPTER 3 People, Possessions and Ourselves: How We Need To See Them

The Good Samaritan
The Rich Fool
The Rich Man and Lazarus
The Pharisee and the Tax-Collector

Significant that Jesus' best-known parable isn't about any-thing abstract or extraordinary but about a very practical example of love. We shall see that Jesus was saying much more than 'Be nice to people.' The parable, when looked at closely, brings out the reason *why* love is essential to any full kind of human life, as well as alerting us to the main obstacle to achieving it.

The *Rich Fool* takes up the fact that all the time we're using the things we have. Whether it's our talents, money, time or other possessions, we know that the quality of our lives depends on the attitude we take to how we use them. So in this parable Jesus paints a portrait as a kind of warning. But he does so in such a way as to evoke a picture of the opposite kind of person. He wants to help us make the choice between two fundamentally different attitudes to our possessions.

The *Rich Man and Lazarus* also turns on a contrast, though not so much between the two main characters as between the Rich Man and the reader – or at least the reader as you or I could be. The Rich Man can't see Lazarus, and so inevitably falls into the sterility of self-centredness. He does so because he won't use the means of seeing that God supplies. The purpose of the story is to help us appreciate that danger and so to make good use of the means of avoiding it.

The story of the *Pharisee and the Tax-Collector* reminds us of the basis of all this. It's so easy to become a machine: a work machine, an administration machine, a money-making machine, or even a 'religious' machine. We know that to the extent we do that we cease to be human. The parable helps us to appreciate the option that we face.

'A man was once on his way down from Jerusalem to Jericho and fell into the hands of robbers; they took all he had, beat him and then made off, leaving him half dead. Now a priest happened to be travelling down the same road, but when he saw the man, he passed by on the other side. In the same way a Levite who came to the place saw him, and passed by on the other side. But a Samaritan traveller who came upon him was moved with compassion when he saw him. He went up and bandaged his wounds, pouring oil and wine on them. He then lifted him on to his own mount, carried him to the inn and looked after him. Next day, he took out two denarii and handed them to the innkeeper. "Look after him," he said, "and on my way back I will make good any extra expense you have." Which of these three, do you think, became a neighbour to the man who fell into the brigands' hands?' 'The one who took pity on him,' he replied. Jesus said, 'Go, and do the same yourself.'[1]

A parable is often like a kiss. It is physical, for it deals with a human action; it can signify deep emotional involvement; and it is simple.

This parable was obviously told so as to centre our attention on a profound and simple action. One man helped another, as he lay in desperate need. We are shown, in practical detail, the help the Samaritan gave. And above all we're shown *why he gave it*.

That must be our starting point: the spotlight the story so insistently directs on a man being 'moved with compassion' and helping. Of course we'll need to ask such questions as 'Why a Samaritan?' and 'Why did the Priest and the Levite not help?' The story, as it is told, demands that we *do* ask such questions. But if we *start* with such questions we run the risk of losing sight of the main impression given by the story: that the whole situation changed in a dramatic climax when someone did not leave another to die miserably by the road as the others had done, but showed compassion to a man who needed it.

The part of the story leading up to the Samaritan is there to help us feel the *need* of his action. Any of us can visualize what it would be like to lie badly beaten up and naked by the side of the road. For Jesus' audience the road from Jerusalem to Jericho was notorious for such occurrences. We can imagine what it would be like to hear the footsteps of a possible helper approaching, see or sense the person looking at us lying there, and then deciding to go on, leaving us to die. All this is rubbing our faces in the lack of humanity, and in the need for it. And then, in just one word, 'compassion', we have what the story has made us want.

In important situations simple words can have an extraordinary power. 'I love you.' 'Well done.' 'Never.' Of course there are occasions when they mean very little, but we know they can mean worlds.

Any of us who tries to tell a story to our friends knows how just one word can give it the shape or point we're aiming at: an ironic sting at the end, a sinister twist, or a moment of truth. To understand how Jesus does this here we need to remember how the Jews had experienced God.

It is true that in a Gallup poll we would probably find that even many Christians believe that in the Old Testament God is experienced primarily as a stern, angry judge. Certainly that was part of the picture: if I deliberately wreck, spoil or twist this magnificent creation, then inevitably I become badly attuned to the goodness in it. But this is simply a consequence *of that goodness*, not a consequence of God wanting to punish or 'get his own back'. The goodness is the main thing. And it arises from a person.

This is how that person made known to Moses the kind of person he is:

Yahweh passed before him and proclaimed, 'Yahweh,

Yahweh, a God of tenderness and compassion, slow to
anger, rich in tender kindness and faithfulness.'
                    (Exodus 34: 6)

Again and again, the Old Testament describes God's relationship with his people as being characterized by tender
kindness. The prophet Hosea, for example, eight centuries
before Christ, when the age of the Greek city was yet to
dawn, felt that God was speaking to his people as a young
man to his intended bride:

I will betroth you to myself for ever,
betroth you with integrity and justice,
with tender kindness (*hesed*) and love.
I will betroth you to myself with faithfulness,
and you will come to know Yahweh.
                    (Hosea 2: 21)

Although that kindness was central to this experience, no
single word could quite catch its richness. So you had to add
words like 'faithfulness' and 'compassion'. They stressed that
God would always be *true* to his people; that his kindness
showed itself in actions that arose from his *feelings* of love
and compassion for them.

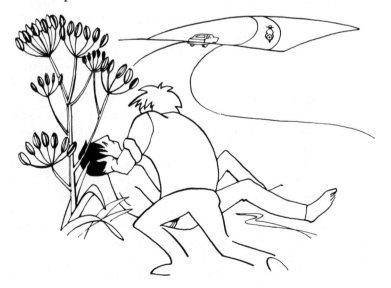

It is here that we meet the word Jesus used as the climax of this parable. 'Compassion' is perhaps the nearest we can get to it in English.[2] Its original meaning involved the gut-reaction of pity: a strong emotion that springs from your whole being. But, in the Bible at least, it wasn't just emotion. It led to love and concrete action. So it meant not only feeling pity and love for someone in need of help, but also the *actions* that show those feelings.

In the Old Testament the word was almost entirely used for God. He showed his 'compassion' for his people by restoring his relationship with them disrupted by their unfaithfulness, and bringing them back from their exile to their own land:

> In excess of anger, for a moment I hid my love from you.
> But with tender kindness (*hesed*) I have compassion for you.
> The mountains may depart,
> the hills be shaken,
> but my tender kindness for you will never be shaken,
> and my covenant of peace will never be shaken,
> says Yahweh, the compassionate.
>   (Isaiah 54: 8, 10)

We can see that he is a God of feeling, close to his people, involved in their situation. He cares strongly about evil. But even that is secondary to his love.

At the time of Jesus it was believed that when the Messiah came God would 'send his compassion to the world'. Indeed one of the titles or descriptions of the Messiah was 'the compassion of God'.[3] So it's not surprising that in the New Testament the word is almost always used to describe the attitude of Jesus, to show that he was acting like God. But there are three exceptions – this parable and two others, and in them Jesus gives us examples of how ordinary people acted in the way most characteristic of God, and he asks his followers to act in the same way. Obviously this extraordinary invitation is the crux of the story. It's like a third-rate football team suddenly finding one of their members at a practice to be a player of top international standard. With all the shock of something hitting you unexpectedly, you feel yourself confronted with a different *kind* of experience, an undreamt-of dimension to life, but one that *you* are being invited to get involved in.

No wonder the lawyer's rather arid question about which group of people you should regard as your neighbour becomes completely turned round.* His conversation with Jesus was about obtaining eternal life. But eternal life isn't a matter of distinguishing one category of person from another. God's invitation is *to live like him*, to share in his creativity with people, with all our heart and our practical actions: to feel and 'do' love and compassion, as he does.

Once we catch this parable at its climax, by seeing how it leads up to the crescendo of 'compassion', and by seeing what that word meant in Jesus' time, we realize that it sweeps us up from the relatively petty questions about categories and asks us to be at home now in a different world, where we live in freedom and fellowship with the God that history had taught the Jews to know: the God who does compassionate actions!

But why does Jesus make a Samaritan the hero of his story, and a Priest and a Levite the villains? Samaritans, as we know, were particularly hated by the Jews of Jesus' time, and the hatred was mutual. To the Jews, the Samaritans were traitors to the true religion, because they followed a false way of worship. The Samaritans, for their part, refused to form alliances with the Jews even when it would have been greatly to their advantage to do so, and they had recently shown their hatred for the Jews by defiling the Temple court during Passover by strewing dead people's bones round it, at midnight.[4]

Jesus seems to choose a Samaritan as the hero of his story to suggest that someone who had no social reason to show compassion did so. The help he gave came not from the almost instinctive reaction we make to a fellow-member of our group but from a deliberate and perhaps long-standing decision to be a compassionate kind of person.

Here we have the other side of Jesus' attempt to show the *real* significance of love, because here he shows not what it

*This point is further discussed in the Notes (page 39).

is but what it is not. He had tried to show what it *is* by using the word 'compassion', which to his listeners suggested God-like. By choosing a Samaritan as the hero of his story, he helps us to see what it isn't. By turning the lawyer's question right round, and by showing that compassion in a *Samaritan*, he indicated that it isn't a cosy little affair of the correct treatment of members of your group but a person's fundamental decision as to his basic attitude to people.

Why did Jesus choose the Priest and the Levite (a Temple servant) as the villains of his story? We have of course to remember that a folk-tale tended to be told in terms of threesomes, and that the first two actors were often there simply to lead up to the climactic third. So the spotlight is on the Samaritan, not on the Priest and Levite, and there is consequently less focus on what they represent or on their motives. Their primary function is to give us a pair of plausible examples of people failing to show compassion.

And this they certainly do. Priests and Levites regularly travelled from Jerusalem, when they had completed their periods of duty at the Temple. Jericho was one of the principal country residences for priests.[5] Although the way Jesus told his story should have helped his audience to realize how heartless these two people were, such heartlessness on their part would have been by no means incredible to his Jewish listeners. For one thing their profession was held in low moral esteem in Jesus' time.[6] And if, as seems probable, the wounded man was an Essene – a religious group that Priests and Levites hated, the heartlessness would have been still more credible.[7] Certainly they are not intended to typify the Jewish religion – in Jesus' time only the Pharisees and Scribes did that. At the same time, they were professionally involved in religious worship. And it is possible that Jesus was using them to re-emphasize the teaching of the prophets: that compassionate action, not mere outward religious observance, is true religion.[8]

What we chiefly need to say about them for the purpose of this story, is that they are there to give us two examples of heartless neglect which would have come across as terribly wrong but entirely credible. And if they were refusing to give help because the man was a member of the Essenes, this would be an added stimulus to the audience to see that neighbourliness can't be settled by juggling with categories but only by you or me looking at the kind of person we are trying to become. And this would have been still clearer in Jesus' concluding question: not 'Which of these three *was* a neighbour?' but 'Which of these three *became* a neighbour?'[9] My obtaining eternal life is forged on the anvil of my deepest decisions about the kind of action I shall do. This is a parable about essential action. Jesus' last word to the lawyer is 'Go, and *do* the same yourself.'

REFLECTION

1. We know that this parable is central to undertanding what it is to be a Christian. It sums up the whole work of Jesus himself. It is about one person helping another in an entirely practical way, with a refreshing freedom from false sentimentality. But in this simple, moving tale, as with so many of his parables, Jesus evokes something very important in his listeners' experience that makes his parable still more profound and appealing: the Hebrew experience of God. So to appreciate what he is saying we obviously need to reflect on that experience and its implications for our view of the world and of ourselves, perhaps by reflecting on some of the biblical texts that articulated it.

2. The parable is there to remind us that those characteristics of God, and therefore of the direction of our destiny, aren't *only* for our wonder and gratitude. The parable turns on a human being *doing* what God does: putting those long-recognized, typical characteristics of God into practice. The coming of the Kingdom of God that Jesus wanted to illustrate through his parables, wasn't about our admiring God as an object, or about our being governed by a higher power, but about our sharing in God's central characteristics and action because we know that to be supremely desirable.

3. Obviously the parable is reminding us that even 'religious' people turn a blind eye to those in great need, and it

helps us to experience what it feels like to find no help in a desperate situation. By making a *Samaritan* the hero, it seems to be helping us to see that what can easily prevent our reacting to people's needs is that we allow the fact that we inevitably belong to certain groups to blind us to the human reality of those who don't. So the parable isn't only telling us that to be a truly compassionate person is to share in the fulness of God's own life; it is also suggesting that to be so involves making a deliberate decision to come to know and love the sheer humanness of people: to respond to the fact that as our brothers and sisters they are one with us. A long way, that, from the relatively comfortable practice of being kind to congenial friends and acquaintances. Sharing in the life and 'compassion' of God involves us asking what we can do to restore by our action a sense that we are fellow human beings, that there is a God-filled glory in the humanity of each of us. Will our civilization survive if this isn't achieved? Has the challenge of this parable ever been so urgent? And, in many ways, have there ever been such great opportunities to achieve what it seeks?

4. 'The North including Eastern Europe has a quarter of the world's population and four-fifths of its income; the South including China has three billion people – three-quarters of the world's population but living on one-fifth of the world's income. In the North, the average person can expect to live for more than seventy years; he or she will rarely be hungry, and will be educated at least up to secondary level. In the countries of the South the great majority of people have a life expectancy of closer to fifty years; in the poorest countries one out of every four children dies before the age of five; one-fifth or more of all the people in the South suffer from hunger and malnutrition; fifty per cent have no chance to become literate.' The World Bank estimates that 800 million people are living in the kind of poverty described here. 'The challenge for the next decades will not be met by an adversary system of winners and losers. . . but only by one founded on human solidarity and international co-operation

amongst all.' (*North-South* (The Brandt Report), pp. 32, 50, 270)*

NOTE

It is disputed whether the lawyer's question was in fact the occasion of this parable. (Most of the conversation with the lawyer is narrated by Matthew and Mark, but without the parable, and there are Lucan stylistic features in it.)

Here it seems important to distinguish two purposes of the parable as we have it. One was to suggest vividly and powerfully that eternal life is obtained by acting with God-like 'compassion'. And the other is to show that, because of that fact, you cannot validly discuss the command 'to love your neighbour as yourself' in the way the lawyer supposed: as sorting out categories.

The first and main aim of the parable would have been achieved whether or not the parable was elicited by the lawyer's question, because the story presents a kind of action as supremely to be imitated and in effect calls it God-like. The story, therefore, did present, in positive, bold and dramatic form, the heart of Jesus' message: that he had come to call people to a share in God's own life, of loving creativity.

The parable's second purpose would have been achieved by implication whether or not the lawyer's question originally elicited the parable. Although it seems very probable that Luke has recast the structure of the parable, so that verses 29 and 36–7 may be his creation at least in part,[10] it seems that Jesus used a well-known rabbinic technique of presenting your central religious insight through pointing to a word-correspondence of a rare word meaning 'you shall love' in 'You shall love Yahweh your God with all your heart, etc.' (Deuteronomy 6: 5) and in 'You must love your neighbour as yourself' (Leviticus 19:18).[11] Obviously he would often have had occasion to put forward this insight, frequently employing this rabbinic technique on these two texts to do so, for example in synagogue worship. This would inevitably have involved him on several occasions in the debate as to who is my neighbour, 'which was in full swing in the days of Jesus'.[12]

*This Report was the result of an independent investigation by a group of international statesmen and leaders from many spheres, headed by the former Chancellor of Germany, Willy Brandt. The eighteen members of the commission came from five continents and different points of the political spectrum.

THE RICH FOOL   Luke 12: 13–21

A man in the crowd said to him, 'Rabbi, tell my brother to give me a share of our inheritance.' 'My friend,' he replied, 'who appointed me your judge, or the arbitrator of your claims?' Then he said to them, 'Watch, and be on your guard against avarice of any kind, for a man's life is not made secure by what he owns, even when he has more than he needs.'

Then he told them a parable: 'There was once a rich man who, having had a good harvest from his land, thought to himself, "What am I to do? I have not enough room to store my crops." Then he said, "This is what I will do: I will pull down my barns and build bigger ones, and store all my grain and my goods in them, and I will say to my soul: My soul, you have plenty of good things laid by for many years to come; take things easy, eat, drink, and have a good time." But God said to him, "Fool! This very night the demand will be made for your soul; and this hoard of yours, whose will it be then?"

So it is when a man stores up treasure for himself in place of making himself rich in the sight of God.'

The occasion that set off this parable was a request for arbitration. The petitioner made it clear that what he wanted from Jesus was a clear-cut decision in his favour. 'Rabbi, tell my brother to give me a share of our inheritance.'[1] A parable was the last thing he was looking for. But it was all he got; and Jesus goes out of his way to explain why he believed it was what the petitioner needed.

The request itself was commonplace enough. The petitioner's father had died, and the estate was now shared between him and his elder brother. The elder brother wanted to keep the estate intact and therefore to have the two of them to continue to live together. Financially, there could be a lot to be said for such an arrangement. But the petitioner wanted to separate off his own share and be independent. A common way of settling such a dispute was to ask a religious teacher to arbitrate. This is what the younger brother asks Jesus to do.

Jesus gives two reasons for declining. One is that he is neither a judge nor someone who divides things up (the Greek word for 'arbitrator' also means 'divider'). His aim is unity, not division; and he has a more profound role to play than just handing out 'answers' which would fail to solve the underlying problem. Only the petitioner can solve the problem: Jesus wants to help him do that.

The solution, Jesus indicates, turns on a choice between avarice and 'life'. If you allow your desire to possess things to get out of proportion, you deprive yourself of a fruitful human life. Although part of the sentence just before the parable is obscure, its general drift is clear. Jesus is suggesting to the man that what is making him seek the division of the property is greed, and that this is damaging his life *as a human being*.

To help the man see this, Jesus tells him a rather special kind of story. Just as science fiction or a detective story quickly introduces the modern reader into its own particular wavelength and kind of interest, so, for Jesus' contemporaries, would the one he was telling here.

By the topic it dealt with and the key words used, Jesus made it clear that the subject of his story is the human person: us in the decisions we have to take: us who have charge of our own destiny and fashion it through those decisions.

Perhaps that is the most fascinating of all topics for men and women everywhere. It was certainly one in which Jesus' contemporaries were supremely interested. And much of that interest centred on a person's choice between wisdom and folly.[2]

Folly was like driving a car with your family in it, when you are wearing totally unsuitable glasses. Human life, like your family in your car, is a marvellous gift entrusted to you. Your responsibility for it demands from you clear-sightedness and wisdom. If you're not going to ruin everything you have, you've got to make sure of seeing things right and using them wisely.

Of course the Jews were by no means the only people who explored the choice between folly and wisdom. To do so is manifestly mere common-sense. But the Jews had increasingly been able to see wisdom's deeper implications. It wasn't just a hedge against disaster. Wisdom, for them, was the rhythm of the universe. Everything that exists echoes the creator's wisdom. By gaining it you enter into the movement of life. By rejecting it you cut yourself off from life.

For the Jew, everything that exists reflected God's strength and wisdom and discernment:

By his power he made the earth,
by his wisdom he set the world firm,
by his discernment he spread out the heavens.
(Jeremiah 10: 12)

Has there ever been, in humanity's history, a vision of the world so radiant, and optimistic? Everything is powerfully directed towards the really good. To be really human is to take our part in this continuing creation. If you take up your human vocation of acting with wisdom and discernment in this great exploit, then this

will prove the life of your soul . . .
You will go on your way in safety,
your feet will not stumble.
When you sit down, you will not be afraid,
when you lie down, sweet will be your sleep.
(Proverbs 3: 22–4)

Jesus' audience would have immediately recognized the man whose picture he painted in his story as just the opposite of that. He does not sleep sweetly, but worries about the future; his way is not safe; his soul is not assured of life. And all because he has opted out of life; he hasn't tried to get things into proportion so that he could live responsibly. He is the very type of the irresponsible man: the man who has rejected wisdom!

The story shows that his wealth was his undoing. The Jews, like anyone of sense, knew that wealth was good provided it didn't enslave you. Their Wisdom literature was full of practical advice about how wealth could destroy that sense of proportion. It listed the sad consequences. There could be ill-humour, irritation, lack of sleep, anxiety, ill-health. There could be pride and harshness with those less gifted than yourself. The underlying cause would be the illusion wealth can give that I am self-sufficient. I stop seeing things as they really are: splendid gifts from God for me to use splendidly. I myself, not God, am the source of what I have; and now I have no difficulty in believing my wealth to be permanent.

Jesus' story supposes that literature's long war on that temptation. Its vivid and pointed aphorisms still speak to us. Riches aren't permanent, it said, but 'a puff of wind'.[3] 'You fix your gaze on dishonest gain, and it is there no longer, for it is able to sprout wings like an eagle that flies off to the sky.'[4]

Riches lead you to avert your attention from the needs of others, so that 'greed shrivels up the soul'.[5] They induce the feeling of self-sufficiency that makes you forget God, and your own limitations. In fact you become your own God ('Let our strength be the yardstick of virtue.')[6] and fall prey to illusory hopes for the future that are 'like chaff carried on the wind, like fine spray driven by the gale'.[7]

These typical mistakes of a person who puts wealth before wisdom are obvious in the man in Jesus' story. His only interest in his wealth is his own enjoyment of it. His confidence in it and his business skills blind him to his own mortality. Owning things and enjoying them are the only things that matter to him.

The story shows the emptiness of this egocentric folly in two ways. Dramatically it shows what happens to the man. What he counted on lasting indefinitely is suddenly wrested from him when he had hardly even completed his plans, and the wealth he had devoted his life to obtaining won't even go to his heirs.

But just as impressive as that person's fate was the *positive* vision of human life offered in their Wisdom literature and evoked by this story. Jesus' story would have conjured that up to them not merely by calling the man a 'Fool' or by the address to the man's 'soul' that was typical of that literature, but above all by values like balance, discernment and practical generosity that his story presupposed.

Today we may have difficulty in recapturing the concreteness and tenderness of those values. The counterparts to folly, wisdom and discernment, can suggest to us just the things of the mind. But for a Jew wisdom meant the *whole* person trying to be true to the world he lives in.

In this parable Jesus was able to count on that more developed idea of wisdom in his audience. It was practical and kindly, and demanded generosity: especially to those in need. The pure selfishness of the man in the story was sheer folly; he forgot that generosity is cherished by God 'like the pupil of his eye'. Turn from the folly of selfishness, Jesus is telling the person who asked for his verdict, and remember what Wisdom tells us:

My son, do not refuse the poor a livelihood. . . .
Do not repulse a hard-pressed beggar,
nor turn your face from a poor man.
Do not avert your eyes from the destitute.
Be like a father to orphans,
and as good as a husband to widows.
Then you will be like a son to the Most High,
whose love for you will surpass your mother's.
(Sirach 4: 1–10)

REFLECTION

1. Jesus knew that his parable would 'work' for the listener only if the story of the rich man was seen against the backdrop he intended for it. This backdrop was a vision of the world as being not an ultimately pointless collection of particles but a marvellous whole filled in all its countless parts by a powerful, wise and discerning God. So before approaching this parable, we need to reflect on that vision of God in the Wisdom literature in the light of which Jesus told his story.

In today's circumstances of massive starvation, of the threat to the economic fabric of many developed countries, and the fear of nuclear war, we may find it more difficult to detect that wisdom. But could these problems help us to realize that God's wise creativeness isn't something that just happens to us but something we must become involved in? Does God want to show the world that wisdom is at the centre of everything *through the witness of what we do about human problems and opportunities*? Isn't this just the challenge given to us by the Kingdom of God?

2. The rich man in the story thought only for himself. The world existed only for his own pleasure. His self-centredness and self-sufficiency are comic and repulsive. We all know our tendency to the same kind of blindness; and we know from seeing selfishness in other people how it 'shrivels up the soul'.

The parable suggests that the alternative to selfishness is wisdom! Wisdom involves trying to see everything and everyone I meet as part of a marvellous, God-filled whole. What can I do to help bring about human fellowship where I live and in the wider world and to help people see for themselves that only this brings joy and the solution to the problems that beset us?

3. We need to feel secure, and we can perhaps unconsciously find our security in our possessions. In a homely, folk-tale way, this story suggests, by the rich man's sudden death, the folly of finding security in them. But again it invites us to contrast this negative, 'folly' side with the positive, 'wisdom' side. Jesus is reminding us of the fact that fills a Christian with awe and gratitude that there *is* security. Those who came to know him well had no doubt of that.

NOTE

Although it is impossible to prove that this parable was spoken by Jesus, quite a lot of evidence suggests that he did speak it. It is true that it is directly concerned with an individual, rather than with

Jesus' main concern of announcing the coming of the Kingdom (to all). But he did warn against the dangers of riches (e.g. Luke 6:24), and he did make pronouncements in the style of Wisdom literature. In addition, the story has Jewish characteristics. There are Hebrew puns in the axiom and in the parable: for example 'life' v. 15 can mean both 'livelihood' and 'the life to come' and 'the benefits I confer on others'; 'crops/produce' v. 17 can mean both 'the harvest' and 'the income from one's heavenly capital'. More importantly, the link between the four 'parts' of the parable would have been most naturally supplied in a Jewish setting by the question of whether one uses one's gifts selfishly or in the service of God and one's neighbour (so obtaining treasure in heaven, in Sirach-type phraseology: Sirach 29: 11). This would tie together the question about the inheritance, the general axiom, the parable itself, and the conclusion.

THE RICH MAN AND LAZARUS
Luke 16: 19–31

'There was a rich man who used to dress in purple and fine linen and feast magnificently every day. And at his gate lay a poor man called Lazarus, covered with sores, who longed to fill himself with the scraps that fell from the rich man's table. Dogs even came and licked his sores. Now the poor man died and was carried away by the angels to be with Abraham. The rich man also died and was buried.

In his torment in Hades he looked up and saw Abraham a long way off with Lazarus close beside him. So he cried out, "Father Abraham, pity me and send Lazarus to dip the tip of his finger in water and cool my tongue, for I am in agony in these flames." "My son," Abraham replied, "remember that during your life good things came your way, just as bad things came the way of Lazarus. Now he is being comforted here while you are in agony. But that is not all: between us and you a great gulf has been fixed, to stop anyone, if he wanted to, crossing from our side to yours, and to stop any crossing from your side to ours."

The rich man replied, "Father, I beg you then to send Lazarus to my father's house, since I have five brothers, to give them warning so that they do not come to this place of torment too." "They have Moses and the prophets," said Abraham," let them listen to them." "Ah no, father Abraham," said the rich man, "but if someone comes to them from the dead, they will repent." Then Abraham said to him, "If they will not listen either to Moses or to the prophets, they will not be convinced even if someone should rise from the dead." '

Once again Jesus takes something from his audience's experience. This time it is a popular story. As writers and other artists have always done, he fashions existing material to his own purposes. A legend about a rich man and a poor man that had been circulating in the East for some centuries could be turned into something that could help those around him to understand what he was saying.[1]

The legend Jesus was adapting went on these lines: You have a rich man and a poor man. The rich man has every good fortune, while the poor man lives and dies in squalor. But after their deaths their fates are completely reversed, for when they go to the kingdom of the dead, the poor man can be seen dressed in royal garments and sitting near the ruler of that kingdom, while the rich man is being punished in a different compartment of that kingdom. In some versions of the story, the poor man lives 'in the garden of paradise in the midst of water fountains', while the rich man 'unsuccessfully stretches out his tongue for the river; he wanted to reach it but could not.' Also we have in the legend someone who comes from the kingdom of the dead to convince a living person about what happens there.

A strange story, certainly: but its point was very simple. It showed, with the imaginative colouring of an oriental story, that the inequalities that are so glaring in life between the very rich (who were liable to have gained their wealth unscrupulously) and the utterly destitute *would one day be evened out*. It was a kind of 'consolation story' for the unfortunate. You may not get good fortune in this life; but don't worry, and don't imagine that those wealthy people who lord it over you will always be the privileged ones: after death everything will be evened out.

Jesus, in his story, *didn't* want to speak about the after-life. He wasn't telling his audience what would happen in the future when they had died. That was just the 'backdrop' to what he wanted to say: the furniture he was taking over from a familiar set.

Once we recognize this, we see that Jesus' story hinges on two main decisions. There is the rich man's decision to be interested only in his pleasures. As a result he couldn't even *see* the beggar at his gate. The other decision (possibly pro-

posed as an excuse for the first) is the one expected of the
rich man's brothers: they wouldn't listen to God's word to
them.

The two decisions are interconnected, because the second
throws quite a lot of light on the first. The rich man knew
what kind of decision his brothers would make *because it
would be like his*. He knew all about people of comfortable
or large incomes not listening to God. The story seems to
make clear that the listening referred to was the weekly
service in the synagogue.[2] That is where, every week, he
and his brothers would have heard 'Moses and the prophets'
read and explained to them. It was the weekly invitation to
respond to God's love for them. This is the kind of passage
a synagogue congregation would be asked to consider:

> (If you) share your bread with the hungry,
> and shelter the homeless poor,
> clothe the man you see to be naked
> and do not turn from your own kin,
> Then will your light shine like the dawn
> and your wound be quickly healed over.
> Your integrity will go before you
> and the glory of God behind you.
> Cry, and God will answer;
> call, and he will say, 'I am here.'
> (Isaiah 58: 7–9)

The parable is about the importance of responding to that
weekly invitation to see the world with *God's* eyes. As an
acknowledged 'son' of Abraham, the rich man often heard
it, and so did his brothers. But it made no difference. There
could be a person outside your gate, crippled, destitute,
starving and wounded, and you wouldn't even realize he or
she was there. Really listening to God meant being prepared
to see things as they are. His word enables us to *see* those in
need. If we don't listen to it, we remain in an unreal world,
spun from our own imagination. We don't live like human
beings at all. Eventually, as in Jesus' story, there is an unbridgeable gap between what we have made of ourselves and
what we would like to be. His story begins by showing us
two people with a *gate* between them, and that makes you

half expect one or the other will go through the gate to the other. By the end of the story that gate has been replaced by unbridgeable chasm.[3] The rich man has made his choice: now it is too late to change.

There is something else Jesus seems to be using that old story to say. The story included miraculous communication between God and people. There it had been just a way of getting the story going: someone from the 'other' world had been shown the rich man and the poor man and what had happened to them. But, in Jesus' version, miraculous communication isn't a handy peg to hang a story on: it's something asked for by the main character, and the request is refused. The rich man asked for it as a way to bypass a difficulty. He knew his brothers wouldn't respond to God addressing them in their weekly invitation to ponder the Scriptures. A miraculous message, he suggested, would get over that difficulty.

Jesus was asking his listeners to consider whether they too, however unconsciously, were making the same kind of request from him. They too were being invited to respond to the word of God: as expressed in Moses and the prophets and now as climactically expressed in him. They said: 'No: if you want us to accept you, you must show us a miraculous sign: something that will make the decision for us: will hand the solution to us on a plate.'

Jesus, like Abraham in his story, turns down the request. Like Abraham he does so because it would not work. When it is a matter of what kind of person I am going to be, there is no substitute for my own decision. Only *I* can find and respond to God. No one can do it for me.

So Jesus turns what had been a soothing bit of escapism for the poor ('you'll get even one day') into a description of the challenge of life for *everyone*. The test of life is to be open-eyed to what is there, and responsive. The alternative is the irrevocable and tragic failure of a human life. The heart of the matter is the stance to life I choose, and my making a real use of the word of God to enlighten that choice.

What about the people in the parable? Abraham seems to rule this place of the dead, when we might have expected God to do that; and in the whole gallery of assorted characters Jesus invented for his parables, Lazarus is the only person who is honoured with a name.

The allusion to Abraham may be of no great significance. In the original story the place of the dead was presided over by Osiris, the Egyptian ruler of that kingdom. And in the versions that were circulating in Palestine, Abraham as the spiritual father of Israel had probably been substituted.[4] If this is the case, Jesus had to name him in order to make the story recognizable. Moreover, it enabled him to make a further point about the unavoidableness of our personal decision. Not only are miracles no substitutes: the same goes for what we belong to. The rich man called for help from his 'father' Abraham; and in Jesus' time many Jews believed that no descendant of Abraham could be lost. Jesus' story makes it clear that even membership of the chosen people is no substitute for choice.

The allusion to Lazarus, too, may have little significance. Orientals, as we know, love to play with names. 'Lazarus' meant 'he whom God helps'. It is possible that in the story Jesus was borrowing from the poor man already had that name: just another detail that went with the 'set'.[5] And, of course, since Abraham was named in the dialogue, the story ran more easily if the poor man was named too.

But it is possible that more is meant by the choice of name. 'Lazarus' was just a different way of writing the name of someone the Jews had come to think of as closely connected with Abraham: Eliezer. Was Jesus alluding to that well-known pair? Eliezer was Abraham's most loyal servant, entrusted with delicate and important missions. Was this another such mission given him by his master: to lie helpless at the rich man's gate to see whether he was keeping the most important obligation of kindness and hospitality to his brethren, just like the mission he had been sent on to Sodom to test *their* hospitality?[6] The crime of Sodom 'was pride, gluttony, arrogance, complacency . . . they never helped the poor and needy . . . that is why I have swept them away.'[7] The crime of the rich man was found, by his reaction to Lazarus, to be the same. And the rich man was 'swept away' from his kin, to a place of punishment.[8]

A difficulty with that theory is that it gives Lazarus a more active and central role than the parable gives him. The parable seems to focus not chiefly on what the rich man does – which is indeed presented as a terrible breach of hospitality, but on his and his brothers' *act of rejection* of God: they wouldn't really listen, wouldn't see what was there, and ultimately it was too late to change.

REFLECTION

1. A Mexican friend once described to me *his* idea of happiness: as 'sitting on my front doorstep, in the sun, eating a bowl of rice'. Judging by the commercials on our TV sets, many of our contemporaries see happiness in more expensive forms! It probably won't be in the form of 'dressing in purple and fine linen and feasting magnificently every day'! It may be having an expensive car or a prestigious job. They bring us comfort and a sense of our importance. The obvious disadvantage with that kind of happiness is that, just like that rich man's fine clothes and feasting, they can make our comfort and our sense of our own importance the only things we're really interested in.

Jesus' story paints a terrible picture of how this can kill the humanity in us, blinding us to the great human need on our very doorstep. St Paul told his friends that he wanted them to be always happy. We may like to compare the kind of happiness that he describes there (Philippians 4: 4–9), which he says can fill our hearts 'with the peace of God', with the kind wanted by the rich man in this parable. What difference does it make to our own character which we choose?

2. We know from our own experience that the impulse to selfishness is strong in all of us. This parable tells us what we have seen for ourselves: that selfishness kills us as human beings. But the parable also reminds us of the cure: opening ourselves to the word that God has always spoken, for example in this parable or in the passage from St Paul.

Probably we've all met people of other religions and of

none who respond to this magnificently – as well as those who don't.

All men and women hear God's word expressed through the physical creation and through human experiences.

The rich man could have had his eyes opened to what life really offers if he had tuned into the experiences his race had had of God as the Scriptures were read to him each week in the synagogue. But he didn't allow them to do that: for him they remained just words.

The people listening to Jesus' parable were in the presence of God's full 'Word', 'the full expression of his being' (Hebrews 1: 3). But instead of something as demanding as responding to a human person, they wanted a short cut. 'Give us a miracle', they said. 'Don't bother us with having to work out who you are. That might make us feel obliged to do things we don't want to do. Give us a miracle, and then maybe we'll see.'

To us, too, the parable points to the same responsibility: that each of us has the unique gift of human personality which self-centredness can kill and God's word can help live. Like the rich man and his brother, I have the word of God read to me each Sunday. Do I listen to what it is saying to me at this moment in my life, to help me see more clearly what I could do? Do I listen to Jesus now present in his community of the Church? I know he lives in the experience and activities of my fellow-Christians. Do I try to be in touch with what they are feeling and doing, as fellow members of a family should? It's true that some of my fellow human beings may well seem the most unlikely people in whom I can experience God. So no doubt did many of the homeless poor to Isaiah's contemporaries. And to the rich man of Jesus' story, Lazarus probably didn't even qualify as a candidate for such a role. Through them Jesus reminds us that if we are to be his followers, we must try to see the world around us as it really is. Listening prayerfully and generously to God's word will help us see it through God's eyes.

3. The sin of the rich man, like Sodom's, 'was pride, gluttony, arrogance, complacency . . . they never helped the

poor and needy . . . that is why I have swept them away.'
Jesus' parable reminds us that we need to reflect on how we
stand with regard to this. The tradition of Christian hospitality may have become restricted in many ways in the modern world. But its gentleness and sheer human appeal can
still inspire us.

4. 'Few people in the North have any detailed conception of
the extent of poverty in the Third World. . . . The combi-
nation of malnutrition, illiteracy, disease, high birth rates,
underemployment, and low income closes off the avenues
of escape; and while other groups are increasingly vocal, the
poor and illiterate are usually conveniently silent.' (*North-
South* (The Brandt Report), p. 49*)
'A truly major effort to eradicate hunger, with its human
degradation and despair, is a political imperative for building
co-operation and solidarity among all people and all nations.'
(Executive Director of the UN World Food Council, January
1979)

NOTES

I. For the first half of this century, most biblical scholars held that
the original parable ended at v. 25. An examination of the folk-
tale background of the parable and the parable's structure has now
led scholars to see the whole passage (vv. 19–31) as basically the
original unit.[9]

II. In rabbinic thought Abraham was the prototype of the virtue
of true hospitality, and Eliezer of the supremely loyal and devoted
servant.[10]

III. Another recent suggestion for the significance of Lazarus' name
does take into account the parable's main focus. It is made in the
context of the view that a parable is a sermon exhortation based
upon biblical texts and can therefore be understood in that setting.[11]
This particular parable could well have been based on two readings
that are known to have gone together in the synagogue readings:
Genesis 15 (the only chapter in the Bible where Eliezer, the servant

* For details about this Report, see footnote on page 39.

of Abraham, *may* be mentioned – the Hebrew text is too corrupt at v. 2 to make this certain) and Isaiah 1. One of the themes of the festival that used these two readings together was the gathering in of the Gentiles and the rebellion and ingratitude of the Jews. Eliezer was a Gentile. This parable, in this theory, would have been a warning that the Jews could be rejected, in spite of their confident reliance on their descent from Abraham, and would see the Gentiles in their place. The description of Lazarus would have been suggested by Isaiah 1: 5.[12] This interpretation would simply be an extension of the one proposed in this commentary.

THE PHARISEE AND THE TAX-COLLECTOR   **Luke 18: 10–14**

'Two men went up to the Temple to pray, one a Pharisee and the other a tax-collector.

The Pharisee, taking his stand, prayed thus: "I thank you, God, that I am not grasping, unjust, adulterous, like the rest of mankind, and, for that matter, not like this tax-collector. I fast twice a week; I pay tithes on all I get." The tax-collector, standing far off, did not dare even to raise his eyes to heaven, but beat his breast and said, "God, show your gracious kindness to me, a sinner."

The latter, I tell you, went home at rights with God, not the former.'

What an extraordinary cast for a story about two people at prayer! It was like choosing a professor and a lumberjack for a two-person commission on higher education.

We see these two people alone, before God, expressing their inmost thoughts about who they take themselves to be. The vivid and sharply contrasted pictures are conveyed to us not just by what they say but just as much by their bodily posture and tone.

First we see a Pharisee who had come to the Temple for either the morning or the afternoon time of prayer. He is standing (a normal posture then for prayer) in the Temple, and he reflects with complacency on his impressive moral achievements. Not just once a year, as the Law prescribed, did he endure long hours without food and especially without drink in that hot climate. He chose to do this twice a week. And while the Law excused him from paying tithes on corn, new wine and oil, since the producer should already have done that, he in fact paid his tithes even on them.

What fine achievements! Jesus' audience would have

thought. It was for just this kind of behaviour that the Pharisees were so admired. And how laudable to remember that all our gifts come from God and to offer him thanks for them!

But even at this stage of the story, there may have been misgivings about this particular Pharisee. Did the excellent things he was doing arise from a real sense of God or from an exaggerated sense of self? A Jewish prayer of thanks (a 'eucharist') was impregnated with a sense of wonder and delight at the greatness of God. You saw God lovingly and creatively active in the whole world. In this kind of prayer you were aware of the giver as much as of the gift, because you saw the gift as typical of the giver: it was proof to you that the whole world is charged with his gracious, kindly presence.

That kind of awareness isn't necessarily expressed in words. In the oldest prayer of thanks known to us it was expressed by the person bowing down in wonder. When words *are* used, we detect it from their tone. But in the prayer of this Pharisee there is no such tone. Its tone is not of wonder but of self-complacency and contempt for others.

The narrow, the negative and the brittle, rather than the broad, warm, positive outlook of prayer.

After the Pharisee has been shown to us, we expect the contrasting member of this ill-assorted pair. Each of them is clearly designed to throw the other into sharper relief. The tax-collector also stands, but at a distance: perhaps in an outer court; and this act of diffidence helps to remind us of the self-confidence of the Pharisee's way of 'standing'.

Another contrast is that one lives virtuously and the other sinfully – but the audience would already know that while Pharisees went to great lengths to keep the Law, someone who became a tax-collector depended for his livelihood on bullying and cheating his fellow-Jews on behalf of the Roman occupying power.

But the most striking and unexpected contrast is the tax-collector's sense of God. This member of an utterly hated profession has the overpowering sense that he stands before God: that his whole being – what he comes to as a person, depends on God. If God, in his mercy, will accept him, in spite of the sins that weigh upon him, then his sense of integrity will be recreated. For him the centre and fountain of all reality is not himself nor aimless chance, but the gracious kindness of God that could overcome even his sense of guilt and inadequacy.

When Jesus ended his story by saying that the tax-collector, and not the Pharisee, went home at rights with God, he was only bringing into focus what his more open-minded listeners could already have realized. Of course it needed a good deal of open-mindedness to envisage the possibility of a traitor being approved by God. But if such a person could be approved by him, then this man was. To deny that was to be insensitive to the whole drift of the story.

But what did Jesus hope his listeners would conclude from this? The parable is obviously not intended to be an outright condemnation of all Pharisees, since it takes only one of them, and Jesus' contemporaries admired the Pharisees too much for such a view to have been considered. Yet it was bound to raise some questions about the Pharisees in the listeners' minds. It scrupulously recorded their great dedication and self-sacrifice. But the evident fairness of the story made it all the more difficult to resist acknowledging that the self-congratulatory tone of that outrageous prayer did ring true to one's experience of *some* of them. That ring of truth would have suggested that self-complacency and the resulting lack of sensitivity to the presence of God were defects that a moral élite, like the Pharisees, is prone to. And since, in the tense situation of the time, the Pharisees were the rejectors and Jesus the rejected, no doubt he was asking his audience to consider whether the Pharisees' proneness to those defects might not do much to explain that rejection. If you were blind to the presence of God in your innermost life, then might you not also be blind to the public coming of God's Kingdom?

If the Pharisees, with their sense of élitism, could be astonishingly blind to the presence in Jesus of a loving and forgiving God, perhaps an equally astonishing ability to perceive that presence could be found at the other end of the spectrum? The choice of a tax-collector for the contrasting figure inevitably brought to mind the most notorious fact about Jesus: that he befriended such people. Might it be that some of those hated and contemptible people had been able to see, through a sense of shame and of need for forgiveness, what God's special presence is really like, while the 'professionally religious' couldn't?

Not, of course, that all tax-collectors could. Jesus wasn't trying to turn the profession into hero-figures any more than he was presenting all Pharisees as villains. But he was trying to suggest something about how people do and do not recognize the presence of God in their lives, and that the shocking spectacle of sinners perceiving it and responding to it was less surprising than it looked.

REFLECTION

We've probably known couples experiencing the breakdown of their marriage because they never really got to know each other. To us, and often to the couple themselves, the marriage seemed happy and secure. It's easy to mistake a sincere feeling of affection for someone, or being kind or protective

towards them, or enjoying their company, for really knowing and loving them as they are. Psychiatrists tell us that this
lack of real communication and mutual knowledge of a couple is one of the main causes of marital breakdown.

Isn't this just the kind of thing we are being shown in this
parable? The Pharisee thought he knew God better than
most. After all he was an acknowledged expert in the theory
and practice of religion. But he had made God into his own
'image and likeness'. He wanted religion to be based on a
set of rules, preferably stiff rules. Well there *are* stiff 'rules'
in religion or in any moral way of life. Is it true to say that
all of us are tempted to reduce that deepest element of life
to some code of rules, in order to tame it? That saves us
from the risks and the strain of committing our whole personality to another.

Yes, the parable tells us, on that basis you can lead what
passes for a virtuous life. But you cannot know God. And
unless someone does a portrait or a parable of what you look
like and you are able to spot the likeness, you may not even
come to know yourself.

NOTES

I. The interpretation of this parable has, over the years, run into
certain blind alleys, and it may be useful to be aware of some of
them.

One blind alley has been created by the second half of v. 14: 'for
everyone who exalts himself will be humbled, but he who humbles
himself will be exalted.' Whether this formed part of the original
parable or not (there are arguments on both sides)[1], it doesn't
provide a catch-phrase that will take us to the heart of the parable,
because *by itself* it easily suggests external acts of pride or of hu-
mility, while the parable invites us into the centre of two people's
inner consciousness, and the parable isn't primarily about the
humiliations or exaltations that may arise from that, but about
what kind of inner attitudes makes a person 'at rights with God'.

II. A second blind alley has been to see the parable as part of Jesus'
blanket condemnation of the Pharisees. But we're more aware
today that Jesus did not deal in such things;[2] and, as we have seen
above, Jesus stresses the positive characteristics of the Pharisees,

and though painting an exaggerated picture of a danger they bring, seeks not to condemn anyone but to help his listeners understand how those characteristics could drown a person's awareness of God in sinners and in Jesus' relationship with them.

III. Another false track has been to understand Jesus' concluding statement that the tax-collector 'went home at rights with God and not the other' as speaking only about forgiveness. It is true that the tax-collector had much to be forgiven for, and that forgiven he was. But what the story is concerned with is *the underlying reasons* for that forgiveness and their practical implications. The tax-collector's prayer is an expression of his awareness that at the heart of life there is a person whose characteristic is 'gracious kindness'. For him, wherever you looked – even in the murkiest corners of his own conscience, that was the chief reality, so that even someone like him could appeal to such a God.

But the Pharisee saw things differently. When he looked at the rest of mankind, like this tax-collector here, he didn't see them in the context of a God of gracious kindness.

The point of the parable, therefore, is to help us answer the question: 'How can I live my life in a *real* relationship with God? How can I be attuned to God?' A genuine relationship between persons demands that we be attuned to one another: that we are able to feel and think and see the world around us through each other's eyes. But God is not just another person, to whom we may care to relate ourselves or not. God is the very ground and fountain of all reality. If you will not recognize and come to the fountain, Jesus is telling us, you will be as parched and soulless as the Pharisee of my story.

IV. The tax-collector's prayer may have used the word which was closely associated with the one used as the climax of the *Good Samaritan*, *Prodigal Son* and *Wicked Servant* parables.[34]

CHAPTER 4 The Time is Now

The Servant Entrusted with Supervision
The Hidden Treasure *and* The Pearl
The Shrewd Steward

Our deepest feelings and values can't be pinned down on a table and labelled with words. So to try to convey them to others we use pictures, images, comparisons, like 'I'm crazy about him,' or 'she's seething with anger.'

And Jesus, too, couldn't give a description of the coming of God that he felt from his deepest being he had to offer: he could only suggest it. 'Come to the feast.' 'Come and work in this most fruitful of vineyards.' 'Come home.' 'Come together again to the one who wants to share his joy with you.' It's not surprising if we find the parables in which he uses those images evocative and moving.*

But we know that we can take someone's love or friendship for granted and let its opportunity pass us by.

In these stories Jesus asks us to consider what kind of opportunity he brings and what we need to do about it if it isn't to slip permanently from our hands.

* I have discussed the *Prodigal Son*, the *Lost Sheep* and *Lost Coin*, the *Workers in the Vineyard* and the *Great Supper* in **Parables for Now**.

THE SERVANT ENTRUSTED WITH SUPERVISION Matthew 24: 45–51; Luke 12: 42–6

'If a master puts one of his servants in charge of providing food at the right times for his house-servants, then that servant is indeed fortunate if his master arrives and finds him doing that. He will certainly promote him to having charge of all his possessions.

But how different it is if the servant says to himself, "I'm sure my master won't be returning here for a long time"! He sets about beating the men-servants and the maids and becomes intoxicated. The master arrives quite suddenly, just when that servant isn't expecting him to. He will punish him with great severity.'

A servant is promoted to butler for the household. He's not that grander kind of steward we shall meet in the *Shrewd Steward* story. The one in this story is still a slave, while the other is a free man who can act in business affairs with the full authority of his master.[1] But he has got power and responsibility for quite a number of people. How he decides to carry out his duties will make a lot of difference to them.

Jesus shows him in a situation where his master may turn up at any moment. True, the butler doesn't always realize that. But that only serves to underline for those hearing the story that it is so. And when the master *does* come, his arrival is like a light being switched on in a darkened room. The butler is suddenly seen for the person he is; it's seen 'in a flash' whether he lives responsibly or not. If he has opted to use his powers responsibly, then he finds that their scope is enormously increased: his master promotes him to 'have charge of all his possessions'. But if he hasn't learnt to use his powers like that, what is left for him? In terms of a folk-tale story about an oriental household, there will be the most ferocious kind of punishment you can imagine.

Folk-tales don't normally take us very deeply into the feelings and attitudes of the participants. They tend not to be individuals, with personalities of their own, but people playing a role: acting as *that kind of person* is apt to. But the situation would have been entirely recognizable to Jesus' listeners. Yes, they were perfectly familiar with that kind of official in any large household. And it wasn't difficult to see how he was meant to be like themselves.

For of course they, like all of us, had power and responsibilities in their families and beyond. And the butler has obviously been drawn, not in order to show that his responsibilities were exceptionally great, or that he had a particularly leading position – he was still a slave – but in order to make it clearer that he was *answerable to his master*.

We're not told how his bullying and drunken rule over the household affected his fellow-servants; the spotlight is entirely on the imminence of the master's arrival. It's as though the master is there, in the audience with us; hidden in the darkness of the theatre from the actor, but on the point of rising from his seat and jumping onto the stage.

It's like that, Jesus seems to be saying, with the Kingdom of God. You're not like a pilot who can put the aeroplane on automatic and let the instruments trundle it across the sky. With the Kingdom, alertness is vital. That's the only kind of use of our gifts and responsibilities that can be fruitful.

And if we do act in that way, then it isn't so much praise that we shall get, or a golden handshake or a halo! *We shall have a full share in our master's authority*. The Kingdom is about God's using his power and authority for all men and women: his making things be, and especially his helping people become their true selves. This kind of creativity, as parents know, is the fullest kind of joy. Our entering into God's joy *is* for us the coming of the Kingdom, if we choose to accept it.

REFLECTION

1. Parable after parable shows Jesus' acute awareness that in him the Kingdom is imminent. The whole world stands on tip-toe. But the world consists mainly of the lives of people: people who become themselves through what they try to do. It is you and I as doing that that Jesus had in mind here. We're not wanted in the Kingdom as mere statistics but as *this particular living person*: talents, purposes, responsibilities, and all. We're not wanted to prop up the stage for a concert in which God is the sole performer. We form part of the orchestra and have the task of helping to make the music which could entrance the world with its truth and joy. The parable seeks to remind us that you can't be an effective member of an orchestra if you forget the conductor, any more than you're likely to be a good steward if you forget that you are a steward.

The alternative, we're shown, is chaos and sterility.

2. Probably inspired by this parable, Paul wrote to the Corinthians: 'People must think of us as Christ's servants, stewards entrusted with the mysteries of God. What is expected of stewards is that each one should be found worthy of his trust' (1 Corinthians 4: 1–2).[2]

NOTES

I. In the early Church this parable was used to warn Christians that 'the Son of Man is coming at an hour you do not expect' (Matthew 24: 44 and Luke 12: 40), and was used particularly to remind especially Church leaders of the responsibilities of their position and above all not to become victims of the illusion that that coming would be long delayed.

Since a preoccupation with the sudden coming of Christ was a chief characteristic of the early Church, where the Son of Man was described by several writers as coming 'like a thief' in the night,[3] several scholars would claim that either the whole of this parable[4] or at least the second half[5] was composed by the early Church.

Their arguments have weight. But in forming an opinion one should, I think, bear in mind the following: that the parable describes a perfectly recognizable bit of Palestinian life and that Jesus spoke about stewardship with regard to our exercising our responsibility to God (the parable of the *Talents*), a conception entirely familiar to his listeners;[6] that he was intensely conscious that all life should now be lived in the context of the dawning of the Kingdom (cf. Luke 12: 54–6; 21: 29–31); that critical and urgent decisions have to be made by all (e.g. the parables of the *Shrewd Steward*, the *Treasure*, the *Pearl*); and that it was his own coming that had brought this urgency (e.g. the *Wicked Tenants*). And in terms of a folk-tale concerning the testing of a steward's sense of responsibility, is it really contrived to have the sudden and unexpected arrival of the master? We know that folk-tales thrive on sharp and dramatic contrasts. And the second half provides not only a contrast of that kind with the first half of the story, but also contains its own: between the riotous and self-confident misbehaviour of the steward and the sudden and unexpected arrival of his master.[7]

II. The story isn't just to build up to a climax of future judgement or punishment. The stress is largely on the *present* situation: that, however appearances may persuade us to the contrary, we *are* answerable for the conduct of our responsibilities: in terms of story, the master is always 'in the wings'. He is 'urgently imminent', like the Kingdom. Of course this leads into final judgement; but it isn't a parable that is simply about final judgement. It's more directly about a final invitation. Will we respond to the reality of the Kingdom now, with its fundamental implications for what we become?[8]

THE HIDDEN TREASURE and THE PEARL   Matthew 13: 44–6

'It is the case with the Kingdom of God as with a treasure hidden in a field which someone has found; he hides it again, goes off happy, sells everything he owns and buys the field.

Or as a trader[1] looking for fine pearls; when he finds one of great value he goes and sells everything he owns and buys it.'

A year or two ago an Australian friend I was showing round London was horrified to find that in a certain London pond tadpoling was forbidden. Soon after he left England to continue his tour of Europe I had a postcard from him to say that in the German towns he had visited tadpoling was *not* forbidden! Having glanced through his frivolous communication, I picked up *The Times*; and my eye was immediately caught by the story of a boy who had been, yes, tadpoling, and, having unearthed thereby an Anglo-Saxon sword, had become richer by its value of £10,000!

Our modern banking methods have reduced incidents like that of the discovery of hidden treasure, and so we may think of the incident described in Jesus' parable as bordering on the fantastic. But in Jesus' time, finding hidden treasure was a recognizable bit of normal life that happened not infrequently.

For centuries keeping your money or valuables safe had been enormously difficult in Palestine. There were as yet of course no banks, and one invasion after another had swept over the country. For most people, in times of national danger, the only thing to do with your money was to bury it as secretly as possible and hope that you would be able to come back and recover it when the worst was over.[2]

So Jesus' audience would have been familiar with this kind of incident. There is a poor day-labourer; he had to scrape together all his possessions in order to buy the field. And buried under the soil is a jar containing silver coins or jewels, the unclaimed nest-egg of some prey to a past invasion. As the labourer ploughs the field, the ploughshare grates against the hidden jar. The man sees the gleaming treasure and quickly buries it again. He *must* have it: it is a prize beyond his dreams. But he can take it safely[3] only if he owns the field, so he sells everything he and his family have got and buys the field.

In the other story we are shown how this time an affluent man did exactly the same kind of thing. He buys pearls from pearl fishers and markets them. The success of his business naturally depends on his acquiring fine-quality pearls from the fishers at a price that will allow a good profit. In this story he finds himself confronted with an exceptional bit of luck. Pearls, used for adornment, especially as necklaces, were then the most precious jewels of the world. There were exceptionally precious ones worth a modern equivalent of a million pounds.[4] Here he finds the opportunity of buying an extremely valuable pearl at a bargain price with the certainty (Jesus' audience would have understood) of selling it for very much more. A huge profit is within his grasp, if he can raise the asking price. Like the ploughman, he finds it will take everything he's got. He decides to take this opportunity of a life-time, sells all he owns, and the pearl is his.

So both stories start as recognizable bits of life, though they don't quite remain that. After that fairly commonplace start, both are given a touch of the fantastic with the fact that both men have to put *everything* into the deal. Without this touch, each would simply be about an unexpected windfall, such as we have on TV when someone wins the football pools. Both men do have the experience of winning a record pools prize; the gain is huge, and it came 'out of the blue'. But unlike the pools winner they've had to put everything they've got into winning it.

That touch of the fantastic helps to keep our attention on that key aspect of the stories, but it also helps in another way too. Jesus was telling the stories to help his audience to understand something about the special coming to them of God's Kingdom. Again and again in their Scriptures God's gift of himself to them is compared to pearls, jewels, or other treasure – sometimes hidden ones.[5] He is showing them a rapid picture, as we might today with a few slides, of how an ordinary person, rich or poor, *can* react when he suddenly finds himself confronted with the chance of a life-time. Are you in that kind of situation today? was the implied question. If so, is that the only way to tackle such an opportunity if one wants to avoid a life-long sense of opportunity missed?

Once again, then, we see Jesus trying to open the eyes of those around them so as to recognize a chance of a life-time and seize it with the decisiveness that the day-labourer and the merchant showed, and which is usually required in real life when such opportunities come.

What action that might be depended then, as it does now,

on the individual or group being addressed by the parable. Human maturity, we are well aware, is knowing who I am: knowing my powers and limitations, what I have and what I want. It is to me as this unique realization of these things that Jesus' plea is addressed, to understand and grasp this opportunity. And only I can decide how, in my present and foreseeable future, I can harness my powers and possessions, my limitations and needs, into the loving, creative work of God in our world.

Some, from Abraham onwards, have felt that they would not be really involved in the Kingdom unless they sold up and moved on. But for most of us the vista we explore when we grasp the magnificence of the opportunity is within the context of ordinary life. Often it is opened up for us by what we see people around us doing.

Perhaps we know someone whose life has been made more deeply human through befriending handicapped people. Or it may have been through their working for a greater sense of justice and community in the neighbourhood or at work. Or the transformation may have come through a greater quality of love and concern for husband or wife and children. Any of these apparently ordinary things may quite suddenly bring us up against the feeling experienced by the day-labourer and the traders of Jesus' stories: that here we are in a world quite different from what we had supposed it to be, so that to live as if it wasn't like that would be absurd.

And yet, as we know, we easily can go on living in that world. Undemanding ruts can be very comfortable. Or they may, as happened with many in Jesus' audience, be *demanding* ruts which pander to our self-importance or achieve for us other selfish aims. Even the most arduous kind of work for others can become like that.

'Old men ought to be explorers', the poet said; and these parables are demanding the same of all who really follow Christ. They show us that really to be involved in God's Kingdom is to be open at all times to experience the un-dreamt of magnificence of what he is seeking to do through us, and to back that with decisive action.

REFLECTION

1. One of the best-loved Christians of our time was C. S. Lewis. It was typical of him that he called his autobiography *Surprised by Joy*, and that the book lives up to its title. These parables are saying that that title should reflect the life of anyone who, in whatever way, discovers the Kingdom.

2. We find an even more powerful sense of joy at having been confronted with such an opportunity in the letters of St Paul. In spite of that turbulent life, full of activity, travel, danger and anxiety, we find in him a serene confidence of having found, and of having *been* found by, a treasure of inestimable value. We may like to read, for example, Ephesians 1: 3–14, or Philippians 3: 5–10 or 4: 4–9.

3. It is interesting to consider what difference it makes if we read the two stories but omit in both cases 'sells everything he owns'. What a different kind of Christianity that would be! Would we prefer it like that? Is it possible to have a real fellowship with Christ without a complete commitment to him, any more than any other deep fellowship among people, like marriage?

4. If we respond to these parables, each of us will 'sell everything' in a way that fits the way in which *we* can get involved in the coming of the Kingdom. Does the great variety in human temperament and circumstances, and the great range of human needs, invite us also to use enterprise and imagination? Are the parables asking us to be not only as determined, but also as shrewd and resourceful, as its two heroes?

5. The Jews found it difficult to think in purely personal terms, and so Jesus' listeners would have seen these parables not only addressed to them as individuals, but still more as addressed to God's people. Many Jews, especially among the religious and political leaders, regarded a serious consideration of the truth of Jesus' claims as too dangerous. It could lead to upsetting the 'status quo': that delicate balancing act

they were conducting with regard to the Roman occupying power by which the Jews were allowed to 'practise their religion' so long as that didn't interfere with how people actually conducted their lives. Does this mean for us today that 'considerations of an ecclesiastical or political or even dogmatic character that prevent our full response to God's call must be given up if we are not to forfeit the name of church of Christ'?[6]

NOTES

I. It has been questioned whether these parables were originally a pair.[7] But the probability is that they were.[8] Contrast and doubling are common techniques even in the simplest works of art. There are many examples in the Gospels of paired parables and symbols, where the same ideas are expressed in different symbols.[9] The practical consequence of this is, of course, that where we are reasonably sure two parables were intended to be a pair, we shall not be responding adequately to the author's attempt to address us unless we take account that he is seeking to communicate with us through these devices. Here it seems to be the *universality* of the teaching being given here: both main 'types', the rich and the poor, wisely follow the same course of action.

II. What are these parables chiefly stressing: the value of the treasure, or its hiddenness; the joy of the finder; the sacrifice the finder makes to acquire the treasure (i.e. what one gives up to acquire it); or the fact that here there is the opportunity of a lifetime that can be gained only by resolute action? It seems clear that all of these are present, but that the last is the point that Jesus was particularly trying to convey. It isn't enough to know what the Kingdom *is*: that it's 'valuable' and hidden; that its finding brings joy and presupposes a willingness for sacrifice. I also need to 'get the feel' of how it relates to how I live: to my quest, through my decisions and actions, for fulfilment. These parables offer us more than general truths. They put us in touch with actual living, dynamic and challenging, to ask us to join it.

THE SHREWD STEWARD   Luke 16: 1–8

'There was a rich man who had a steward, and charges were brought to him that he was wasting his goods. He called him and said to him, "What is this I hear about you? Surrender the account books, for you can no longer be steward."

And the steward said to himself, "What shall I do because my master is taking the stewardship away from me? I am not strong enough to farm and am ashamed to beg. I know what I shall do so that when I am put out of the stewardship they may receive me into their own houses."

So, summoning his master's debtors one by one, he said to the first, "How much do you owe my master?" "A hundred measures of oil", was the reply. And he said to him, "Take your bill and sit down quickly and write fifty." Then he said to another, "And how much do you owe?" "A hundred measures of wheat", was the reply. And he said to him, "Take your bill and write eighty."

Then the master commended the dishonest steward for his wisdom, because the sons of this age are wiser than the sons of light judged by the standard of their generation.'[1]

Jesus' listeners could easily have visualized this story[2] of a Palestinian rogue. You had a landowner, with an agent administering his land. This agent, or 'steward', would have been a man of considerable social standing in his locality. Not only the servants in his master's household, but even the steward of the household himself would have had to treat him with deference, for *their* status was roughly that of slaves, while the agent was a free man.

The agent's main job was to rent out his master's land to neighbouring farmers. This was quite a lucrative position. Besides his salary from the landowner, he would have had fees from the farmers for drawing up the rental contracts. And most of them would probably consider it wise to 'grease the palms' of such an important official with a present from time to time.

A man with such power in the local community, and with so many opportunities of malpractice, could obviously attract critics. This particular agent finds himself facing accusations by local people that he has been wasting his master's goods. His master charges him with this, and he makes no attempt at denial. Instead of taking the expected course of having the man jailed and forced to pay compensation, the master is merciful and merely fires him. 'Surrender the account books,' he orders him, 'for you can no longer be steward.'

From the moment of this order the agent legally has no authority to act on his master's behalf. But he still has to go back to his office, get the account books, and bring them back to his master. And on his way back to his office to do that, the full realization of his present plight strikes him. Every avenue to a tolerable way of life now seems barred to him. The only glimmer of hope comes from the fact that so far news of his dismissal has not spread, and he still has those symbols of his authority, the account books! Why be in too much of a hurry to return them? Why not keep them in his hands for as long as he dares, and make use of the authority they seem to give to make provision for the rough times that now certainly lie ahead?

With all the speed of someone who knows that the news of his dismissal could explode at any moment, he immediately 'summons' the farmers. They don't get a friendly request to 'drop in some time', but a 'summons' from this important official, acting apparently with all the authority of the landowner himself. He summons them in, one by one – it would be unsafe to have them talking to one another, and addresses them with all the authority of his former position: 'What do you owe my master?' The terms of the leases are that their annual rent is a fixed amount of the produce, and each verbally confirms what is already on the account in the agent's hands. In so much of a hurry that he doesn't even address them as 'Friend' or 'Sir', he rattles out his order to each to change the entry in the account to a lesser amount.

Naturally the farmers are delighted. 'A splendid fellow, this agent,' they would tell their friends. 'He even talked the old gentleman into a big cut in my annual rent.' High praise of the agent's enlightened and big-hearted action would soon be round the village; and that evening many a toast would be drunk to him.

News of these celebrations soon gets to the landowner, who by now has had the accounts returned to him by his sacked agent. He can now check for himself that the amounts have been fraudulently reduced. Yes, once more he has been cheated by this rogue, and he must decide what he will do about it.

Have him arrested? He isn't so sure. He isn't a vindictive man, as the restrained way he had reacted to the earlier mishandling shows. Also, is he going to dash the euphoria and celebrations in the village induced by what the local people have understood as his own big-heartedness by announcing that it has all been a mistake?

Instead, he decides to back his steward's action and to praise him for the deftness and wisdom he has shown in a tight corner. Then, in the last words, Jesus takes the story and points it at his listeners; he tells them that those who want to belong to God's Kingdom ('the children of light') should take a lesson from, of all people, that dishonest steward! What was he suggesting we should learn from him?

A large clue to the answer is provided when Jesus says that the master praised the dishonest steward 'for his wisdom'. One meaning of the word 'wisdom' was cleverness and skill deployed in self-preservation,[3] which was of course exactly what the steward had shown in his dismissal crisis. But it was also used for the sense of urgency and wisdom the followers of Jesus needed to have now that the Kingdom was coming.[4] They too, like the steward, have wasted their master's goods. They too must, by urgent and wise action, earn their master's 'praise': a word that suggests in the New Testament the approval of God at the judgement.[5]

It is *possible* that the parable is also asking us to consider that the steward entrusted 'everything to the unfailing mercy of his generous master who, he can be confident, will pay the price for man's salvation.'[6] It is true that the master is merciful in only firing the steward, rather than having him imprisoned when he discovers he has been wasting his goods, and that his decision at the end of the parable to praise rather than punish also shows mercy. It can also be argued that the steward must have relied on the mercy of his master to have cut the debts at all, because swift discovery was certain. But perhaps the main impression given us as we read the story is one of deft (and unscrupulous) action, not reliance on mercy; and the master's concluding comment gives no clear clue that the steward's wisdom included a perception that his hope lay in his master's mercy.

REFLECTION

1. We know that the Kingdom of God isn't something that merely comes to us: it is an activity, God's activity in the world, that we are asked to become involved in. This is the enterprise in which we are invited to make a fruitful use of our abilities.

This parable seems to underline the need we have of shrewdness as we try to make this fruitful use of our powers. Most of us can be pretty clearsighted when we want to be and are able to make prompt use of the resources we have. If Christianity seems rather a tame and marginal affair to many of our contemporaries, could that be largely because we haven't troubled to make a shrewd alert use of our responsibilities as Christians? We were founded to be a 'kingly, priestly and prophetic People'.[7] Do we speak out (or even try to understand) the injustices in our world, like the 'prophets' we're meant to be? Do we make a full use of the world as God's marvellous creation, like 'kings'? Do we make the presence of God available to our contemporaries in the way we live, as 'priests'?

2. The parable also underlines the urgency of the action required. I remember a fifty-year-old saying to me contentedly some years ago: 'Life is so long!'

Life *may* be long for you and me. We may have many years yet. Though it's up to us, of course, how profitable they may be.

It's probably true that Jesus felt overpoweringly that the time was now for God's people. Is the same true for God's people today; is our time a special opportunity, which only we can seize?

Perhaps it isn't chiefly a question of taking a decision *now*, before it is too late, but the fact that a decision *for the Kingdom* isn't the kind you can palter with: that it must be either fullhearted commitment, or false and fruitless. And of course there *will* be a time for each of us when we shall have to 'surrender the account book'.

3. Our master, as the parable of the *Talents* showed, is one who loves to praise and delight in the fruitfulness in us that his gift enables, and which our shrewd use of that gift can achieve.

NOTES

I. The reconstruction of the story here comes from a writer who knows Palestinian rural life intimately and who is a biblical scholar as well. In spite of the fact that there are different reconstructions, as we shall see, it is widely agreed that the main general point that Jesus seems to be making with this parable is 'the crisis of the imminent arrival of God's Kingdom. . . . It is a warning to the hearers to take stock of their actual situation, to see how they already stand under divine judgement, and to take action now.'[8] A rough modern equivalent (though it omits the theological overtones) might go like this:

There was a certain labour racketeer who had grown rich on sweetheart contracts and illegal use of the union pension fund. One day he found that the FBI was tailing him and he began to suspect that there was no escape for him. So what did he do? Carefully, he put a large sum of money away where no one could touch it and then faced trial. He was duly convicted and after he had exhausted all his rights to appeal, he finally served a sentence in the Atlanta Federal penitentiary. Having served his time, he took his money and moved to Miami Beach, where he lived happily ever after.[9]

But is this urgent and essential action to do with the use of money? The more common opinion is that the original parable finished at either 8a or 8b;[10] but some hold that it had its conclusion, and its application, in v. 9:[11] 'So I tell you this: use money to win your friends, and thus make sure that when it fails you, they will welcome you into the tents of eternity.' For them, of course, the parable is to do with *the prudent stewardship of money.* But even some who hold that v. 9 didn't belong to the original parable believe that it is not just about prudence shown in the face of a crisis in general, but 'prudent use of material wealth with regard to it'.[12] But this latter view largely rests on the belief that the steward was shrewdly forfeiting profits that were coming to *him* – a view that now seems untenable. There are good arguments for a whole range of often mutually conflicting views on this and on the inclusion of v. 9, and I doubt whether they can at present lead us further than to a position of 'maybe'.

II. *In what way was the manager dishonest?* One view is that the debts were in fact money, not goods, but expressed in terms of goods so as to disguise the fact that the agreements evaded the prohibition of usury by the Law of God. What the steward did was to cut this interest from the debts. His crisis-situation impelled him to give up this claim on the debtors and thereby to 'obey' the Law of God.[13] By doing so, he hadn't deprived his master of anything that should really have been his. In these circumstances it wasn't so strange that his master praised him. We must note that he praises him for his 'shrewdness', not for his dishonesty as such.

Some would add that the interest was the steward's cut, so that he wasn't depriving his master of anything, but merely forgoing his own profit or commission.[14]

Against both these views it has been objected: (1) it is much more probable that the debts were genuinely produce rather than money. One of the three ways of renting land was to pay a fixed portion of the crop to be grown. And (2) according to Jewish Law the steward couldn't have charged interest without his master knowing about it; and the steward *would* have received a salary: i.e. he wasn't forfeiting his own unofficial salary.[15] Therefore the steward was depriving the master of what was legally and morally his, and so one has to find a different reason for the master's praise of him. I have followed this view in the commentary, and given the reason for the praise put forward by its proponent. It may well seem rather contrived; but I don't know of one that better fits the facts as we seem to have them.

CHAPTER 5

The Choice

The Children in the Market Place
The Wicked Tenants

Jesus wanted people to join him if they loved him and what he stood for. And we know that we can love another person only if we are sensitive to their personality and to their deepest wishes and feelings.

These parables ask whether we will choose to love and follow Jesus. In the *Children in the Market Place* an eager invitation to friends to share in happiness was turned down. In the *Wicked Tenants* story, Jesus reminds us how often that has happened to the invitations God has sent. Will it really happen again now, when God has sent Jesus himself?

THE CHILDREN IN THE MARKET
PLACE   Matthew 11: 16–19; Luke 7: 31–5

'What description can I find for the men of this generation? What are they like? They are like children shouting
to their friends as they sit in the market place:

> We played the pipes for you,
> and you wouldn't dance;
> we sang dirges,
> and you wouldn't beat your breasts like mourners.

For John came, neither eating nor drinking, and they
say, "He is possessed." The son of man came, eating
and drinking, and they say, "Look, a glutton and a
drunkard, a friend of tax collectors and sinners." Yet
wisdom has been proved right by her offspring.'[1]

We see the slums of Harlem or Palermo, or children lying
on the ground helpless with starvation on our television sets,
and we ask: 'Who permits this evil? who is responsible?' And
perhaps we say, 'Oh, governments, administrators, and circumstances.' But each of us knows perfectly well where
much of the blame must fall. We are 'the generation' that
never gets round to changing these circumstances and in-
sisting that political leaders and administrators put the right-
ing of such things near the top of the list, instead of near the
bottom.
   When Jesus began his parable by saying that he would try
to describe 'the generation', his listeners knew that he would
be reminding them of their corporate responsibility for what
was happening. The phrase echoed so many reminders of
that sort in their Scriptures. 'A stubborn and unruly generation, a generation with no sincerity of heart, in spirit unfaith-
ful to God' was only one example.[2]
   Then, through a picture from everyday life in the village

street, Jesus tries to get them to see what is wrong. Some children sitting in the market place want to get their friends to join in their play. They don't mind whether it is 'weddings' or 'funerals', so long as their friends will join in the fun. So they play 'wedding' music, for their friends to break into the round dance used for weddings; but that was no good. Then they try 'funeral' music, for their friends to beat their breasts and foreheads in time with the music like mourners at a funeral, but again no response. Whatever kind of musical game the children offered them, their friends refused the invitation.

'Isn't it just like that now, with you?' Jesus is asking. 'John and I come in ways that should have convinced you that it is God who has sent us to you' – and for 'come' he used a word by which the Scriptures referred to the coming of God or his special messengers.[3] 'John and I, in our different ways, announce to you that the Kingdom is upon you. But, like the friends of those children, you turn down the invitation for no apparent reason. In whatever way God offers you a manifestation of his loving presence and invitation to you, you won't come in on this vibrant and marvellous event, but mutter on the side-lines about "possession" and "evil companions".'

The parable, therefore, is about a failure to accept the invitation of the Kingdom, even when offered in such different forms.

REFLECTION

1. The Pharisees' reaction to this parable could have been indignant: 'We deaf to God's invitations and messengers! Insulting and absurd! We're his chosen people and we follow his Law.'

Yet, as we know, they were deaf. And we also know why. They assumed they had God sized up, so they knew the kind of way he would act when he came to them. They had reduced God to their own image and likeness, so that it was like playing a great symphony to a person who chooses to appreciate only trash.

The sadness of it is brought out by the contrast between the merriment that the children wanted to enjoy with their friends and the contemptuous refusal of John's and Jesus' critics.

Once again, then, religion has been the pretext for a smallness of mind and self-complacency that has throttled opportunity: *the* opportunity of all human history. Are we open to God, or only to a man-made travesty? We know that we can let religion become no more for us than a means of bolstering up our own tastes, emotional needs, or even prejudices, and how easily any of us can lapse into this. But do we *use* that awareness to consider such things as God's love of *all* people, that all are his children and our sisters and brothers, and that life is in fact nonsense unless seen in terms of the fellowship of God's own family?

2. The parable reminds us of the endless variety of God's ways of addressing us. It shows us that we aren't alive to God's presence if we fail to catch something of its manifoldness. Are there people who send shivers up our self-righteous spines among those we know? If there are, should we ask ourselves whether we are as dead to the splendour of the Kingdom as those Jews were?

NOTES

I. This commentary accepts the view that the children who invited their friends to play correspond to Jesus and John inviting the Jews to respond to the good news about the Kingdom. For reasons mentioned in Note II, this seems more probable than the opposite view: that the children inviting their friends to play correspond to the Jews, who invited John the Baptist to celebrate (but instead he fasted) and Jesus to fast (but instead he gave parties for tax collectors and sinners). Either way, the parable is saying much the same thing: the Kingdom has been and is being offered to you *in very different ways* that transcend your preconceptions, but you won't respond to any of them.

This is obviously what the parable is saying if Jesus and John are the children inviting their companions to take part. But if it is the Jews who are issuing the invitation, it still comes to the same thing because the point then would be that they insist on Jesus 'mourning' (observing the religious fasts) and John 'dancing' (observing the religious festivals) *because the Jews refused to respond to the particular way* the Kingdom was being offered them by each of these special messengers of God.

II. The chief argument for the view that it is *the Jews* who are asking John and Jesus to 'dance' and 'mourn' respectively is that in the sequel it is the Jews who 'speak' and complain, so should we not say that it must also be they who 'speak' and complain in the parable (the Greek gives the identical word for 'speak' in each case)?[4] But if our view is correct that John and Jesus are those who 'speak' first, then we might well expect that those who refused their invitation should 'speak' second: to explain *why* they refused. 'Why *should* we accept the invitation of someone clearly possessed or of someone who disqualifies himself from being regarded as a sound religious teacher by dining with that kind of person?' The main difficulty against accepting the Jews as the inviters, however, is that it seems to strain metaphor rather far to suggest that the Jews tried to 'call the tune' for John and Jesus.[5] It is true that 'they asked both John and Jesus to observe traditional customs', namely 'that they should take part in feast when people had their festivals and fast when decent people fasted',[6] though this isn't given prominence in the Gospels. Either view is logically possible. The decisive question seems to be whether we regard the children's invitation as having more the atmosphere of *a positive and urgent opportunity* than as a mainly tacit demand to conform to custom.

If the view proposed here is correct, the introduction to the rhyme must be admitted to be clumsy. We would expect, 'This generation is like children sitting in the market place *to whom* their friends shout.' It is possible that that *was* the original reading, which was changed to the present clumsy form by the mistaken insertion of one letter in front of the Aramaic word for 'friends', so that it ceased being the subject and became a dative-object.[7]

III. Matthew and Luke have Jesus saying that 'the son of man' came. It is possible that here 'Jesus used a term which might have seemed to be merely a self-reference' (i.e. he seemed just to be saying 'I') 'but which in reality conveyed a deeper meaning.'[8] The arguments are very complex, and since John and Jesus are placed alongside each other as God's messengers, it seems clear that the pre-eminence of Jesus is not here being emphasized.

IV. With regard to the last sentence of the passage, it is reasonably clear that Luke has better preserved the original: 'Wisdom has been proved right by her *offspring'* (not 'actions', as in Matthew). It tells us that the wise plan of God has proved right. But it is difficult or impossible to tell whether it is proved right *by* her children: i.e. those who have accepted Jesus; or *despite* (as the underlying Aramaic may mean) her children: i.e. in spite of the fact that those who should 'by nature' follow her as God's chosen people in fact reject her.

THE WICKED TENANTS   Mark 12: 1–11;
Matthew 21: 33–44; Luke 20: 9–18

'A man had a vineyard and put it in the charge of some
vineyard workers. After a time, he sent a servant to the
vineyard workers to take the fruits of the vineyard. But
they seized him, beat him and sent him away empty-
handed. He sent another servant, and him they killed.
He had one more to send: his son. He sent him last.
They seized him and killed him.'[1]

Jesus was in Jerusalem. The rapidly mounting hostility from
the Jewish authorities made him aware that his final clash
with them could not be long delayed. In this situation he
told a story of a vineyard. This time it wasn't a homely
detail of life in the Galilean uplands that caught his eye and
sparked off his story. But the spark may well have been
provided by something he saw. There in Jerusalem, in the
Temple where he was teaching, a branch of a vine, made of
gold, trailed down the columns of the portico.[2] For him that
branch must have been deeply evocative. More than seven
centuries ago a prophet had called God's people 'a luxuriant
vine yielding plenty of fruit'.[3] For Isaiah, at about the same
time, the image suggested a love affair:

> Let me sing to my friend
> the song of his love for his vineyard.
> (Isaiah 5: 1)

God treats his vineyard like a lover, with tenderness and
delight:

> Sing of the delightful vineyard!
> I, God, am its keeper;
> every moment I water it
> for fear its leaves should fall;
> night and day I watch over it.
> (Isaiah 27: 2–3)

But the love-affair had always been a chequered one. God had offered to his people his love and care, but often they have rejected him:

> I would like to go harvesting there, says God.
> But there are no grapes on the vine,
> no figs on the fig tree:
> even the leaves are withered.
>   (Jeremiah 8:13)

In that relationship the vineyard was a symbol of love and tender care and happiness. Always God wanted 'to give her (his people) back her vineyards, and make even the Valley of Misfortune a gateway of hope.'[4]

Now that Jesus had come, would God's love for his vineyard be rejected? Whether or not he told his story under that trailing golden vine-branch, both that branch and the Temple itself must have been especially poignant to him. They spoke confidently of a thousand-year promise for which the next few weeks or even days would be critical. He must try to warn his audience of the situation. So he told this story.

Those listening to Jesus would have been in no doubt who was meant by the maltreated servants. Again and again God had sent prophets to his people to call them back to him. 'Day after day I have persistently sent you all my servants the prophets. But they have not listened to me, have not paid attention.' That patient offer of close friendship had been ignored. The prophets who had so persistently been sent to bring that offer had been rejected and persecuted. Jesus' story paints the same picture: his vineyard-owner, too, tries again and again, but his servants suffer a similar fate to the prophets. His patience is not yet exhausted, and he tries one last time: he sends his son. But he too is rejected.

Might this story not help his listeners to recognize their situation? They knew well enough that their people had so often rejected and maltreated God's messengers. They knew that their God was loving and patient with them. Could this man who was speaking to them, Jesus of Nazareth, himself be a prophet, the *last* prophet? Could this be God's last throw: his final attempt in the greatest of all his messengers, his 'son'? Were the machinations going on in the city to secure this man's death the final rejection of this people's destiny?

Especially against the background of the image of the vineyard, it was to anyone who would really listen a deeply moving plea. They knew what God said in Isaiah about his people:

> What could I have done for my vineyard
> that I have not done?
> I expected it to yield grapes.
> Why did it yield sour grapes instead?
> (Isaiah 5: 4)

The parable helps us to see Jesus in the last weeks of his life. Probably his making the climax of the story the sending of the owner's son arose from his acute consciousness, not only of his own immediate danger, but above all of being completely and profoundly at one with all that God wanted to do for his people. It wasn't a matter of a title – 'Son of God', for example, wasn't thought of as a title for the Messiah at that time. It was, rather, that in what he had done and said his listeners had been confronted with the goodness and authority of God with a unique immediacy.[5]

This was Jesus' strong and tender appeal to God's chosen people to open their eyes before they swept aside this final approach.

REFLECTION

The parable can help us wake to our own situation. We too are sent prophets (in the Church as a whole, but particularly where we live), whom we are inclined to reject. God is present in the Church, guiding us, through Christians every-where. An essential part of every Christian's vocation is to be God's mouthpiece, his prophet, speaking out about the situations we are responsible for in the light of his truth.

We do not hear God mainly through dramatic or promi-nent figures, but very often through the ordinary people around us who through God's Spirit in their lives and their prayer speak profound, enriching truths which we need to listen to if we are to flourish in God's love. But we, like Jesus' audience, may find it more convenient to reject them.

CHAPTER 6

Impressions

Anyone who has had to write a reference for a friend apply-
ing for a job knows the limitations of precise description. If
only we could have that employer with us and chat, say over
a glass of beer, about our friend. We'd like to talk about our
impressions: impressions built up from a close experience of
our friend. In comparison with that, the letter we write may
seem only to skim the surface.

Isn't it the same with the parables? There was a time, of
course, when the Bible was regarded as a kind of armoury
of definitions ready to be shot at the opposing camp. Now
we're much more ready to stand and stare; to let ourselves
reflect upon the people and events that we see there.

Who is this story-teller? It would be good to share impressions. Since here I can only offer my own, I think my first
one is that of welcome: that insistence on welcoming everyone who would come, in spite of the scandal that was bound
to cause to 'religious' people. And when great offence was
taken and protests were made, we find not the barrage of
argument we might have expected, but stories! The father
in the *Prodigal Son* story ignoring insult and the great wrong
done to him, and having 'compassion' on his son. The joy
of the shepherd, and of the woman who had lost her coin.
The insistence of the host that there *would* be a great party,
even if those originally invited declined to come.

To anyone open to Jesus, these stories must have made
sense in terms of what they *saw* of him. They had seen the
compassion and the joy and the insistence on celebrating.
But it must have been obvious, even to those who hated
him, that those stories, and others like them, weren't just
about Jesus. Even his most implacable opponents could realize that he was deliberately recalling what *God* does. The
stories were so strongly reminiscent of how God helps the
weak and oppressed, is kind and compassionate, tangibly

and repeatedly shows his generosity, seeks out the lost, gathers his flock, invites to a feast.

Don't we have here an extraordinary fusion of the blatantly mundane and a nation's thousand-year experience of its God? Not woven into frenzied tirades, eloquent sermons or elaborate lectures. Just stories.

They're brief stories, sometimes witty stories, and always close, like Jesus himself, to people as they really are. No doubt those children who wouldn't play could have been seen in any village market place. The story of the Pompous Pharisee, suitably told, would have been good for a laugh in the right company. But the parables aren't biting. Obviously a story-teller of that imagination and skill could have been mordantly satirical; and we know there was no lack of provocation. But we find no trace of an attempt to batter the enemy, only an appeal to him or her to think again.

So we have this balance between humour and urgency. The stories observe sympathetically the ordinary goings on of life: the sower scattering his seed, sometimes among those tough, dry thorns; the man roused up at night by the unexpected guest; the woman kneading dough; and the labourers grumbling about their differentials. But always the everyday scene is pregnant with the coming of God. For Jesus everything seems to have 'spoken' of that. Evidently he had a profound inner consciousness that in a very special sense he was acting as God had promised to do when he finally 'came' to his people: that he was, as the *Wicked Tenants* story suggests, God's 'son'.

Everywhere he looked he could evidently see the urgency, the joy and the dependability of that coming. In the labourer in the field, hoping that his spade might strike a hidden hoard; or in that well-dressed merchant dreaming of making a fortune; or in a disgraced steward, or a butler, or even in a mustard seed! In this varied and vivid world, the seed was growing towards harvest, the great dragnet was already sweeping through the water. You had to choose: weed or wheat?

Wheat grows to harvest, weed is burnt as useless; that was the choice he had to bring. And don't we have here again that sense of balance or humanity: a balance between the conviction of the crucial importance of the message, and the absolute respect for the person. Jesus doesn't insist menacingly, eyeball to eyeball, 'weed or wheat?'. He only tells a story. 'Here I am,' he suggests, 'You see what I'm like and what I am doing. Does this story help you to see that harvest is near, and that you must decide whether you'll be part of it?'

At the risk of seeming to trivialize, I'd ask whether the thing we're specially recapturing today about Jesus is his style. In the parables he seems to be saying: 'Here's shepherding; here's finding the lost; here's compassion. What do you think of it? Are the sheer style of it, and the attitudes that expresses, God-like?'

We know very well that showing compassion is largely a matter of how you do it: whether there is spontaneity, warmth, perhaps courage, and the attitudes you show to the other person. We've all, alas, observed how 'religion' can quench style. We're kind as a 'moral duty'. We worship like this or act like that, because people expect us to. And if we're not careful these useful aids become ends in themselves and we become dead to people in their needs and their variousness. The parables make it clear that that was neither God's way nor Jesus' way. The father in the *Prodigal Son* story didn't run to embrace his son because he'd worked out in the quiet of his study that that was his moral duty. Still less did he do what was expected of him by those outraged villagers.

So the style of the Kingdom, if we may talk in those terms, seems to be one of an exceptional openness to life: to its quirks and contrariness, to its people and their ways, to God and what he wants to achieve through and for his people, and for all men and women.

Isn't a large part of the Christian agenda that we try to recapture this more fully? The Christian churches have come a long way recently in breaking out of their formalism and inwardlookingness. The parables show us the compelling attractiveness of the Kingdom. May we increasingly come to share in its spirit so that others have a real opportunity of stumbling for themselves on this treasure, hidden in the field.

ENDNOTES

Abbreviations used in these endnotes:

Bible versions:
JB — *Jerusalem Bible*
NEB — *New English Bible*
RSV — *Revised Standard Version*

Books:
K. Bailey, *Poet* — K. E. Bailey, *Poet and Peasant*. Grand Rapids 1976

J. Derrett, *Law* — J. D. M. Derrett, *Law in the New Testament*. London 1970

J. Jeremias, *Parables* — J. Jeremias, *The Parables of Jesus*. London 1963

E. Linnemann, *Parables* — E. Linnemann, *Parables of Jesus*. London 1966

I. Howard Marshall, *Luke* — I. Howard Marshall, *The Gospel of Luke*. Exeter, 1978

TDNT — G. Kittel and G. Friedrich, ed., *Theological Dictionary of the New Testament*. Grand Rapids 1964–76.

Periodicals:
JBL — *Journal of Biblical Literature*
JTS — *Journal of Theological Studies* (new series)
NT — *Novum Testamentum*
NTS — *New Testament Studies*

ZNW   *Zeitschrift für die*
                       Neuetestamentliche
                       Wissenschaft

The Friend at Midnight (pp. 4–8)

[1] The text given here is that of K. Bailey, *Poet*, p. 122 but adapted so as to go into prose.

[2] K. Bailey, ibid., p. 122.

[3] K. Bailey, ibid., p. 123.

[4] Commentators differ as to the weight we should give to the friend's plea about the door already being closed, etc. K. Bailey sees them as 'weak considerations . . . so unthinkable, they are humorous' (ibid., p. 124); J. Derrett, 'The Friend at Midnight: Asian Ideas in the Gospel of St Luke', in C. K. Barrett, ed., *Donum Gentilicium*, (Oxford 1978), p. 82; and J. Jeremias, *Parables*, pp. 157–8, estimate the inconvenience more highly.

[5] *A Man for All Seasons* (London 1960), Preface, p. xii.

[6] The Hebrew people's interest was not in abstractly conceived qualities of their God but on the qualities he had proved himself to have in their experience of him (cf. H. Wildberger, in E. Jenni, ed., *Theologische Handwörterbuch zum Alten Testament* (Munich), vol. i (1971) column 184.

[7] Cf. K. Bailey, op. cit., pp. 124–5; and I. Howard Marshall, *Luke*, p. 464. J. Dupont and J. Jeremias disagree with this view.

[8] *RSV* 'importunity'; *Good News Bible* 'not ashamed to keep asking'; *JB* 'persistence'. *NEB* keeps the interpretation open: 'the very shamelessness of the request'. 'Importunity' is suggested by J. Jeremias, *Parables*, p. 159, and W. Ott, *Gebet und Heil* (Munich 1965), p. 99.

[9] Cf. I. Howard Marshall, *Luke*, p. 465; and K. Bailey, *Poet*, p. 133.

[10] J. Derrett, art. cit., p. 83.

[11] J. Derrett, ibid, p. 81 (and see p. 82).

The Unjust Judge (pp. 9–14)

[1] This text assumes that except for Lucan editing in v. 6a, vv. 2–8 are basically original (cf. I. Marshall, *Luke*, pp. 670–1; and David R. Catchpole, 'The Son of Man's Search for Faith (Luke xviii 8b)'. *NT* 19 (1977), pp. 81–104). V. 5 'Will damage my reputation', cf. J. Duncan M. Derrett, 'Law in the New Testament: the parable of the Unjust Judge', *Studies in the New Testament* (Leiden), vol. i, p. 43–5 (accepted by subsequent commentators, eg. Zimmerman and Marshall). V. 5 'The help she is entitled to'; 7 'Give help in their need'; 8 'rescue them': the same word in each. It can also mean justice in the sense of punishment, revenge or reparation. Here it seems to mean 'give them the help they need, particularly the full

coming of the Kingdom and rescue from persecution'. Cf. H. Zimmermann, 'Das Gleichnis vom Richter und der Witwe', in R. Schnackenburg et al., ed., *Die Kirche des Anfangs* (1978), p. 87; and I. Howard Marshall, *Luke*, p. 674; V. 7 'he who limits the punishment for their sins': many very different interpretations have been given for this clause. David Catchpole has recently shown its Old Testament meaning in this context (art. cit., pp. 92–101).

[2] Monetary cases were tried by a single judge rather than by a tribunal.

[3] R. Deschryver, 'La parabole du juge malveillant', *Revue d'histoire et de philosophie religieuses*, vol. 48 (1968), p. 36.

[4] Leviticus 25: 17.

[5] *TDNT* ix, p. 445 (G. Stählin).

[6] Jeremiah 7: 6.

[7] *TDNT*, art. cit., p. 450, n 86.

[8] Zimmermann, art. cit., p. 87.

[9] Ecclesiasticus/Sirach 35: 12–14.

[10] For other examples see David R. Catchpole, art cit., pp. 93–8.

The Unmerciful Servant (pp. 15–22)

[1] J. Jeremias, *Parables*, p. 210.

[2] Cf. David Catchpole, 'The Son of Man's Search for Faith', *NT*, 19 (1977), pp. 93–8.

[3] Outside this and two other parables of Jesus (the *Good Samaritan* and the *Prodigal Son*), it is always used in the Synoptic Gospels 'to describe the attitude of Jesus and it characterizes the divine nature of his acts' (*TDNT*, vii, p. 553). In the Old Testament the Hebrew verb that mainly underlay the Greek word used here had come also to be used preponderantly of God (E. Jenni, ed., *Theologische Handwörterbuch zum Alten Testament*, (Munich), vol. ii (1975), column 766 (H. J. Stoebe)).

[4] *TDNT*, v, pp. 561–3 (F. Hauck).

The Servants Entrusted with Money (pp. 23–28)

[1] For this text and the most thorough exegesis of the parable in its two versions, cf. A. Weiser, *Die Knechtsgleichnisse der synoptischen Evangelien* (Munich 1971), pp. 226–72.

[2] In his subsequent study of some of Luke's parables, G. Schneider finds that even if one accepts that the version of the parable inherited by Luke at least reflected the problem of the delay of the coming of the Lord, nevertheless the main stress in the version inherited by Luke (though not in Luke's own), was the duty to make a profit from the 'money' entrusted to you (*Parusiegleichnisse im Lukas-Evangelium* (Stuttgart 1975), p. 42).

[3] I. Howard Marshall, *Luke*, p. 704.

[4] J. Jeremias, *Parables*, p. 61; and I. Howard Marshall, op. cit., p. 706.

The Good Samaritan (pp. 31–39)

[1] Some hold that the parable (as opposed to the conversation with the lawyer) was not spoken by Jesus, but was created by Luke himself: particularly G. Sellin, 'Lukas als Gleichniserzähler', *ZNW*, 65 (1974), pp. 166–89, and 66 (1975), pp. 19–60. His comparison of the structure of the conversation (vv. 25–8) and the parable, etc. (vv. 29–37), pp. 19–20, makes it clear that Luke has made the structures of both correspond. But his contention that the story itself must be ascribed to Luke is unconvincing: (1). There is a strong Palestinian content to the parable (cf. particularly C. Daniel, 'Les Esséniens et l'arrière-fond historique de la parabole du bon Samaritan', *NT*, 11 (1969), pp. 71–104); several details strongly suggest that the wounded man was an Essene. (2). Sellin's positive argument about the meaning of the parable (that you must treat Samaritans as your neighbour if they keep the law of love) rests on a too legalistic interpretation of 'compassion' and 'mercy' for the New Testament. (3). This makes it easier for him to reject the view that the parable presents a shift of standpoint (from 'Whom should I treat as my neighbour?' to 'How do I become a neighbour?'). But if, as I argue in *Parables for Now* (p. 87), the parable of the *Prodigal Son* was basically spoken by Jesus, radical shifts of viewpoint – again in a parable largely about compassion – are hardly surprising in Jesus' parables. His central teaching was in any case precisely a radical shift on the question of love and compassion, as well as on earning/accepting the gracious gift of 'justification'. (4). Sellin and others also contend that 'a basic law of parable-telling' forces us (p. 24) to identify ourselves *throughout* with one person: here, the wounded man, so that the question must remain that of knowing whom we should treat as neighbour. Again, one could point to the *Prodigal Son* as a clear exception to this 'law'. What seems to me to undermine this law here is the explosively sudden mention of 'compassion'. Up to that point our involvement had in fact been *twofold*: primarily, certainly, in the situation of the wounded man, but also partly in why fellow-Jews were so heartless. From that point, *both* involvements are continued: it is *the priority between them* that is shifted. On 'became a neighbour', cf. note 9 below.

[2] The Hebrew words for 'tender kindness' and 'compassion' have been studied quite recently by H. J. Stoebe in E. Jenni, ed., *Theologische Handwörterbuch zum Alten Testament* (Munich), vol. i (1971) columns 600–21; and vol. ii (1975) columns 761–8 respectively. With regard to the Greek equivalents in Jesus' time, cf. *TDNT*, vii, p. 552 (H. Köster).

[3] References given ibid., p. 552.

[4] In AD 6; cf. J. Jeremias, *Parables*, p. 204.

[5] I. Howard Marshall, *Luke*, p. 448.

[6] 'Idolaters, adulterers, lovers of money, proud, lawless, luxurious, abusers of children and beasts': Testament of the Twelve Patriarchs, Testament of Levi 17 (cf. E. Linnemann, *Parables*, p. 139 note 7).

[7] C. Daniel, art. cit., pp. 97–100.

[8] Cf. Isaiah 58: 6–9. The point has been emphasized recently by L. Ra-

maroson, 'Comme "Le Bon Samaritan" ne chercher qu'à aimer', *Biblica*, 56 (1975), pp. 535–6.

[9] The lawyer asked 'who *is* my neighbour?' Jesus makes clear that the real question is 'who *became* a neighbour?' This fact has been obscured by mistranslations in the *JB* and *NEB* (the *JB* has 'proved himself a neighbour' and the *NEB* 'was a neighbour'. *Luther's Bible* translates correctly with 'sei gewesen'). Cf. L. Ramaroson, art. cit., pp. 533–4.

[10] G. Sellin, art. cit., *ZNW*, 66 (1975), especially p. 35–8.

[11] Cf. W. Diezinger, 'Zum Liebesgebot Mark: 12–34 und Parr', *NT*, 20 (1978), pp. 81–3.

[12] *TDNT*, vi, p. 316 (H. Greeven).

The Rich Fool (pp. 40–46)

[1] Cf. J. Derrett, 'The Rich Fool', *Studies in the New Testament*, vol. ii (Leiden 1978), pp. 99–120.

[2] On the Wisdom literature background to the parable, cf. Egbert. W. Seng, 'Der Reiche Tor', *NT*, 20 (1978), pp. 136–55.

[3] Psalm 39:6;

[4] Proverbs 23:5

[5] Sirach 14: 8–9.

[6] Wisdom 2:11

[7] Wisdom 5: 14.

Rich man and Lazarus (pp. 47–55)

[1] The story was originally proposed as the background to the parable by H. Gressmann, *Vom reichen Mann und armen Lazarus* (Berlin 1918), pp. 62–8. There is an abbreviated version in T. Lorenzen, 'A Biblical Meditation of Luke 16: 19–31', *Expository Times*, 87 (1975–6), p. 41; cf. also K. Grobel, ' . . . "whose name was Neves" ', *NTS*, 10 (1963–4), pp. 373–82.

[2] Otto Glombitza, 'Der reiche Mann und der arme Lazarus', *NT*, 12 (1970), pp. 176–6.

[3] F. Schnider and W. Stenger, 'Der reiche Mann und arme Lazarus', *NTS* (1979), pp. 273–83, see this as the key-point for understanding the parable. This seems to be an exaggeration. It should be blended with the equally important point about how the rich man could have *seen* who was the other side of the gate: through *really* listening to the Scriptures. The article doesn't seem to give sufficient structural importance to this second major point.

[4] Cf. K. Grobel, art. cit., p. 380.

[5] Ibid., p. 381.

[6] According to the Babylonian Talmud, *Sanhedrin* 109a–b.

[7] Ezekiel 16: 49–51.

[8] This theory has been argued by J. Derrett, *Law* (1970), pp. 78–99.

[9] Though it is agreed that v. 31 is now 'couched in terms of resurrection, rather than simply a messenger from the dead' (I. Howard Marshall, *Luke*, p. 639). On the parable's basic unity, cf. J. Jeremias, *Parables,* p. 186; I. Howard Marshall, op. cit., pp. 633–4; F. Schnider and W. Stenger, art. cit., pp. 273–83. C. F. Evans is much more sceptical about its unity ('Uncomfortable Words', *Expository Times*, 81 (1969–70), pp. 228–31).

[10] Cf. L. J. Rabinowitz, 'The Study of a Midrash', *Jewish Quarterly Review*, 58 (1967–8), pp. 143f.

[11] By C. H. Cave, 'The Parables and the Scriptures', *NTS*, 11 (1964–5), pp. 374–87.

[12] Cf. C. H. Cave, 'Lazarus and the Lukan Deuteronomy', *NTS*, 15 (1968–9), pp. 319–25.

The Pharisee and the Tax-Collector (pp. 56–61)

[1] T. W. Manson, *The Sayings of Jesus* (London 1949), p. 312, and E. Linnemann, *Parables*, p. 64, would say that it was not part of the original. I. H. Marshall, *Luke*, pp. 680–1, and L. Schottroff, 'Die Erzählung vom Pharisäer und Zollner', in H. D. Betz, ed., *Neues Testament und christliche Existenz* (Tübingen 1973), pp. 457–50, feel obliged to leave the matter open. Its form is very Jewish, but it is found in two other places in the Gospels (Matthew 23: 12 and Luke 14: 11); cf. *TDNT*, viii, p. 16 (W. Grundmann).

[2] T. W. Manson, op. cit., pp. 309–10.

[3] F. F. Bruce, 'Justification by Faith in the Non-Pauline Writings of the New Testament', *Evangelical Quarterly*, 24 (1952), p. 67 and note 4.

[4] There has recently arisen another blind alley, but it is perhaps mainly confined to scholars. It is that 'Jesus' listeners will not have felt the prayer of the Pharisee to be hypocritical arrogance, but a genuine prayer of thanks for God's gracious guidance' (E. Linnemann, *Parables*, p. 59). This view is shared by equally influential scholars (like J. Jeremias, *Parables*, p. 143). It is based largely on the contention that there is a very similar prayer of a pious scribe. But it has been pointed out that that prayer (quoted by Linnemann and Jeremias) does not label all besides the person praying 'grasping, unjust adulterers'; cf. L. Schottroff, art. cit., pp. 448–51. As Schottroff points out (pp. 456–7), the listeners would have to be prepared for the conclusion of the parable by feeling morally alienated from the Pharisee in his relationship with God. The view also seems to ignore the importance of tone and posture as well as just words and the close contrast established through these between the two people portrayed (e.g. the 'standing' of one makes important by contrast the 'standing' of the other). Linnemann rightly sees that the parable is about counting on God's grace rather than on Law (p. 63), but she doesn't accept that the first part of the parable is to move the reader towards this view; for her the direction of the parable is hidden until both portraits have been painted. Another important consequence of her not giving the first of the two portraits sufficient weight is that she overstresses the fact that the tax-collector is

in a state of sin. The parable is *more* about a true awareness of God than about this resulting from an awareness of sin as her explanation seems to suggest.

The Servant Entrusted with Supervision (pp. 63–66)

[1] *TDNT*, v. pp. 149–51 (O. Mitchel).

[2] *TDNT*, viii, p. 542 (K. Rengstorf).

[3] 1 Thessalonians 5: 1f; 2 Peter 3: 10; Revelation 3: 3; 16: 15.

[4] D. Lührmann, *Die Redaktion der Logienquelle* (Assen 1969), p. 70.

[5] E.g. G. Schneider, *Parusiegleichnisse im Lukas-Evangelium* (Stuttgart 1975), p. 28.

[6] 'In the Greek version of the OT Bible the word "to be a servant" is the most common term for the service of God, not in the sense of an isolated act, but in that of total commitment to the Godhead' *TDNT* ii, p. 267 (K. Rengstorf).

[7] Amongst recent writers who favour the ascription to Jesus are A. Weiser, *Die Knechtsgleichnisse der synoptischen Evangelien* (Munich 1971), pp. 161–225; J. Jeremias, *Parables*, pp. 55–8; and I. Howard Marshall, *Luke*, pp. 534–42 ('the possibility of elaboration (in vv. 45ff) cannot be dismissed out of hand').

[8] A. Weiser, op. cit., pp. 204–13 compares the many views, and then advances what I think is the right solution.

The Hidden Treasure and the Pearl (pp. 67–72)

[1] J. Jeremias, *Parables*, p. 199.

[2] J. Jeremias, ibid., pp. 198–200; E. Linnemann, *Parables*, pp. 98–9; and C. W. F. Smith, *The Jesus of the Parables* (Philadelphia 1975), p. 64.

[3] Cf. J. Derrett, *Law*, pp. 1–13. But the moral or legal right of the labourer to remove the treasure is not of importance for the meaning of the parable.

[4] R. Schippers, 'The Mashal-character of the parable of the Pearl', *Studia Evangelica* II (1961, published 1964), pp. 236–7.

[5] Cf. B. Gerhardsson, 'The Seven Parables in Matthew 13', *NTS*, 19 (1972–3), p. 24.

[6] C. W. F. Smith, op. cit., p. 65.

[7] Especially by O. Glombitza, 'Der Perlenkaufmann', *NTS*, 7 (1960–1), pp. 153–61.

[8] Cf. J. Dupont, 'Les paraboles du Trésor et de la Perle', *NTS*, 14 (1967–8), p. 409.

[9] Examples given in J. Jeremias, *Parables*, p. 90 and note 6.

The Shrewd Steward (pp. 73–79)

[1] This is basically the text given by K. Bailey, *Poet*, p. 95, in the light of his own suggestion of 'surrender the account books' (p. 97) and of J. Derrett's 'judged by the standard of their generation' (*Law*, p. 79, note 1).

[2] The reconstruction given here is that of K. Bailey, op. cit., pp. 88–102.

[3] *TDNT*, vii, p. 484 (G. Fohrer).

[4] Cf. Matthew 25: 2, 4, 8f.

[5] *TDNT*, ii, p. 587 (H. Preisker).

[6] K. Bailey, op. cit., p. 107.

[7] The three main roles of a Christian, according to the Second Vatican Council; cf. *Dogmatic Constitution on the Church*, chapters 2, 9–12.

[8] B. Lindars, 'Jesus and the Pharisees', in C. K. Barrett, ed., *Donum Gentilicium* (Oxford 1978), p. 56.

[9] Norman Perrin, *Rediscovering the Teaching of Jesus* (London 1967), p. 115.

[10] Cf. J. Fitzmyer, *Essays on the Semitic Background of the New Testament* (London 1971), pp. 166–70.

[11] E.g. I. Howard Marshall, *Luke*, p. 622. There are plenty of other views as to the function and division of Luke 16: 1–13 (e.g. that 8–9 are an indignant exclamation implying 'of course not!' R. Merkelbach, 'Über das Gleichnis vom ungerechten Haushalter', *Vigiliae Christianae*, 33 (1979), pp. 180–1).

[12] J. Fitzmyer, op. cit., p. 177.

[13] Cf. J. Derrett, *Law*, pp. 48–78; and *Studies in the New Testament*, vol. i (Leiden 1977), pp. 1–3.

[14] Cf. I. Howard Marshall, *Luke*, p. 615.

[15] Cf. K. Bailey, op. cit., pp. 89–93.

Children in the Market Place (pp. 81–85)

[1] I have tried to reconstruct so far as possible the original text from Matthew's and Luke's versions. *The double question from Luke*, rather than Matthew's introduction: a semitism – semitisms abound throughout the text. '*To their friends*', rather than 'to the others' or 'to each other': cf. H. Sahlin, 'Traditionskritische Bemerkungen zu zwei Evangelienperikopen', *Studia Theologica*, 33 (1979), pp. 77–80. '*Beat your breasts like mourners*', rather than Luke's 'cry': cf. O. Linton, 'The Parable of the Children's Game', *NTS*, 22 (1976), p. 162; and I. Howard Marshall, *Luke*, p. 300. On the mourning custom, cf. *TDNT*, iii, p. 845 (G. Stahlin). '*A glutton and a drunkard, a friend of tax collectors and sinners*', rather than omit 'a friend of tax collectors and sinners', as Stahlin (ibid. pp. 82–3) suggests as perhaps advisable, on the grounds that the charge that Jesus was 'a glutton and a drunkard' alludes to the unruly son who according to the Old Testament should be stoned (Deuteronomy 21: 18ff Masoretic text), so the accusation of being 'a friend of tax collectors and sinners' would seem relatively tame after that. But although in the mouths of the Jews, that could be so, in

the mouth of Jesus it was only a repetition of what had been said about him, so that two originally separate charges of originally different intensity could have been listed. 'Proved right by her offspring', rather than 'proved right by all her children' as in Luke: cf. O. Linton, pp. 164–5 (with self-contradictory misprint in his conclusion).

[2] Quotation from Psalm 78: 8. Other instances: Deuteronomy 32: 5, 20; Judges 2: 10; Psalm 95: 10; Jeremiah 7: 29; cf. I. Howard Marshall, op. cit. p. 299; and TDNT, i, pp. 662f (F. Büchsel).

[3] TDNT, ii, pp. 667–71 (J. Schneider).

[4] O. Linton, art. cit., pp. 171–7.

[5] Stressed by Dieter Zeller, 'Die Bildlogik des Gleichnisses Mat 11: 16f/ Lk 7: 31–5', ZNW (1977), p. 254.

[6] O. Linton, art. cit., pp. 177 and 175.

[7] H. Sahlin, art. cit., pp. 78–9.

[8] I. Howard Marshall, op. cit., p. 303.

The Wicked Tenants (pp. 86–89)

[1] This is the text reconstructed in French by M. Hubaut, La parabole des vignerons homicides (Paris 1976), p. 131, after deleting what he considers to be later accretions that occurred either through subsequent allegorization (e.g. most of Mark 12: 1 and the whole of 4) or for purposes of early Christian polemics against the Jews (Mark 12: 6 ('Beloved son'), 7, 9 and 10). I assume here that the parable was in some form by Jesus and was allegory. This parable as we have it in the three Synoptics has clearly been extensively edited by them to adapt it to the interests of their readers. We therefore have to ask whether a parable spoken by Jesus himself underlies it, and, if so, what it said. Scripture scholars tend to think that a parable of Jesus *does* underlie the present texts, but they differ about the form it took. Their views are influenced by whether they think that Jesus' parables were just stories or whether they could be allegories. One very influential view, particularly represented by J. D. Crossan, in 'The Parable of the Wicked Husbandmen', JBL, 90 (1971), is that Jesus' parables were not allegories. With regard to this particular parable support is found for this view from the similar passage in the Gospel of Thomas, which has no overt allegory and which 'must be taken as the earliest stage of the tradition' (art. cit., p. 461). The difficulties with this view are: 1. that subsequent research seems to suggest that the Gospel of Thomas passage is extensively dependent on Luke (Hubaut, op. cit., pp. 132–4. and B. Dehandschutter, 'La Parabole des vignerons homicides', in M. Sabbe, ed., L'Evangile selon Marc (Louvain 1974), pp. 203–19); 2. There is no compelling evidence for the claim that Jesus couldn't have composed an allegory. If, as the three Synoptics say, he was speaking here in the Temple, the imaginative spark that gave rise to it could well have been something he observed there (which was likely to be symbolic) rather than possible or actual incidents of Galilean life; 3. A very large proportion of the details of the synoptic versions have clearly allegorical significance. If these ver-

sions represent, as now seems probable, earlier traditions of the story than the Gospel of Thomas, it seems highly unlikely that a totally unallegorical story should receive so much strong allegorical colouration so consistently and so quickly (especially given the fact that we find allegory in earlier versions we can deduce from the synoptic texts); 4. This allegory would, in Crossan's words, 'drive towards participation rather than information', just as much as would a story.

Another view holds that the parable 'is a realistic description of the revolutionary attitude of the Galilean peasants towards the foreign land-lords' (J. Jeremias, *Parables*, p. 74). Because the landlord is living abroad, the tenants can take liberties with his servants. They kill the son because they assume that the owner is dead and that the son has come to take up his inheritance. If they kill him, the vineyard becomes ownerless, and under certain circumstances an inheritance may be regarded as ownerless and the first claimant gets it. In this interpretation Jesus' listeners were to see themselves as rebellious tenants, whose rebellion would lead to the vineyard being given to 'others'. By analogy with similar parables, these 'others' would be 'the poor'.

There are several difficulties against this interpretation: 1. A Galilean audience would have realized that the rebellious tenants would be evicted by the indignant owner. But they wouldn't have regarded a foreign capitalist or his action with sympathy. Hence the story as such wasn't well calculated to move them to perceive the wrongness in their rebellion; 2. It presupposes that verse 9 was included in the story as Jesus told it, but it seems more likely to have been a very early creation of the Christian community under the influence of Isaiah 5: 1–7 (cf. Hubaut, op. cit., pp. 54–6 and 127–8); 3. In spite of the great amount of learning and ingenuity that has been expended on defending the view that the story was intended by Jesus, not as allegory, but as a story drawn from recog-nizable everyday life (especially by J. M. Derrett, *Law*, pp. 286–312), some of the important details of the story can be made to fit with that view only by using an excess of ingenuity. For example, this interpretation has the tenants suppose that the true owner is dead or may have assigned his rights to the son, so that by killing him *they* would acquire the vineyard (by a claim of undisputed possession) rather than it remaining the property in law of his still living father. J. Derrett has subsequently given evidence for the view that the parable could have been intended as an allegory, in his *Studies in the New Testament*, volume ii (Leiden 1978), pp. 92–8.

[2] A suggestion first made more than seventy years ago, and developed by M. Hubaut, op. cit., p. 139.

[3] Hosea 10: 1.

[4] Hosea 2: 15.

[5] Cf. A. Weiser, *Die Knechtsgleichnisse der synoptischen Evangelien* (Munich 1971), p. 51; and M. Hubaut, op. cit., p. 136.